THE ANGLICAN FORMULARIES
AND
HOLY SCRIPTURE

Reformed Catholicism and Biblical Doctrine

by

Peter Toon

Brynmill / Preservation Press

typeset by The Brynmill Press Ltd
printed in the USA

ISBNs USA 1-879793-09-1   978-1-879793-09-5
ISBNs UK 0 907839 92 4   978 0 907839 92 7

British Library Cataloguing in Publication Data: a catalogue
record of this book is available from the British Library.

Contents

Preface

This short essay, commending the historic Formularies of the Anglican Way, appears at this particular time (late summer 2006) to coincide with two events. First, the publication of a special, indeed unique, Anglican Book, and secondly, a deliberate searching by a growing number of Episcopalians [Anglicans] in North America for the fullness of the Anglican Way.

The book is an English classic and has been out of print for some time. It is in fact two books, bound as one—*The Homilies*. It dates from the middle of the sixteenth century, is described in Article XXXV of The Thirty-Nine Articles of Religion and is referred to in "The Order for Holy Communion" in *The Book of Common Prayer* (1662). The printed sermons are a primary source of the knowledge of Reformed Catholicism for they expound its worship, doctrine and morals for the ordinary church member to receive. Edited and introduced by Ian Robinson, the volume is published in the U.K. by Edgeways Books and in the USA by the Preservation Press of the Prayer Book Society. It is truly a treasure.

The Anglican Way in North America is currently in a distressing condition and as such it has become a major concern of, and problem for, the whole Anglican family around the world. One of the reasons for the crisis and distress in the USA is that the mainline denomination known as The Episcopal Church has forsaken much of its own heritage in worship, doctrine and discipline. Thus both within its present membership, and amongst those who have in recent times left its membership, there is a desire to become acquainted, or familiar, or more familiar, with the historic and theological foundations of the Anglican Way. I offer this essay to these persons as one way for them to begin to find their Anglican roots, which will be also, their biblical roots.

I wish to express my appreciation to various colleagues and friends who have commented on drafts of this essay. Though I write it during the time when I am the President of the Prayer Book Society, USA, it is not an official statement from the Board of the Society, but an essay by me which is cordially supported by the Board. I hope you profit from it and, more so, from the reading of *The Homilies*.

Trinity VI; July 2006   *Peter Toon*

CHAPTER ONE

The Anglican Way in the new Millennium

Into the 1960s, and perhaps well into the 1970s, the Churches of the Anglican Communion were basically united. They used the same *Book of Common Prayer*, based on the English edition of 1662; had an Episcopate recognized by all (ordained and consecrated by means of *The Ordinal* of 1662); were based on the authority of the Scriptures for faith and conduct (and reading the King James Version); administered faithfully the two Gospel Sacraments; recited and taught the truths of the Creeds; proclaimed the Gospel of the Father concerning his Son, the Lord Jesus Christ, for the salvation of sinners; were involved in mission of varied kinds, and lived in "bonds of affection" based upon a common heritage and long friendships. Differences were discussed at Lambeth Conferences every ten years and, in general, the "bonds of affection" remained strong despite problems and challenges.

Since the 1970s, especially in the West, a working unity based on a common center and comprehensiveness in terms of churchmanship has been gradually eroded due to a series of different and not always related factors—e.g., the introduction of forms of liturgy alternative to those in *The Book of Common Prayer*; the absorption of the doctrine and the outworking of civil and human rights to challenge received Christian moral teaching; the sexual revolution with its roots in the 1960s undermining the institution of marriage and the duty of procreation; the great mobility of people taking them away from their roots; and the emphasis on instant gratification, relevance, simplicity and self worth, making traditional discipline and holiness seem obsolete.

In the history of The Episcopal Church since the 1960s it is possible to see a most definite change of direction and character adopted in the late 1960s and pursued relentlessly since then (see my *Episcopal Innovations, 1960–2004*, for a description of this). Similar but less obvious change has occurred in the Church of England and the Anglican Church of Canada, both of which, like The Episcopal Church, have decreased dramatically in active membership in the last fifty years. So the crisis deeply felt by Anglicans in the new millennium has been developing for some time.

The authentic Anglican Way

In what follows, I shall seek to present the Anglican Way as it has been traditionally understood and described, and as, probably, it is still viewed by the majority in most of the Anglican Communion today. My aim in what immediately follows is to set a context in which the doxological and doctrinal basis of the Anglican Way of the past, for the present, and into the future can be described and then explained in later chapters.

1. It is specifically the **Anglican** Way. The Church of England's Latin name is *Ecclesia Anglicana* and so the Church of England may be called, "The Anglican Church." Likewise, Churches created and formed from this Church, or from Churches related by origin to this Church, are called Anglican, and the worldwide fellowship of them has been called in recent times, "The Anglican Communion of Churches." Since this whole family of national Churches or regional provinces has developed from one Church, itself a National Church, it has been the tradition to speak of the Anglican Way as a unity and thus as a jurisdiction, or a branch of, the one, holy, catholic and apostolic Church.

2. It is the **Reformed Catholic** Way. Anglican Churches claim to be Reformed Catholic in character. This associates them with two separate entities—the Roman Catholic Church (or The Catholic Church as it calls itself) and the (Protestant) Reformation of the sixteenth century. The Anglican Way was not created in the sixteenth century since the *Ecclesia Anglicana* had existed for many centuries; but it took particular shape, form and content in the middle of the sixteenth century. The Church of England reformed the medieval form of Catholicism which it inherited, and it reformed itself by the Gospel, and specifically by the Gospel as it had been rediscovered by Luther and Calvin through St Paul's doctrine of justification by faith alone through the grace of God in our Lord Jesus Christ. Unlike Protestant Churches in Switzerland and Scotland, however, the Church of England maintained the Catholic Order of the Threefold

Ministry, government by bishops (under the godly monarch), and the Catholic tradition of an authorized liturgy.

3. It is a **Scriptural** Way. The Church of England committed itself to the absolute authority and sufficiency of Scripture in all matters concerning salvation from sin and into everlasting life. This commitment included from the beginning the availability of the Bible in English in printed form in every parish of the land. In its *Thirty-Nine Articles of Religion* the supreme authority of Scripture was stated with clarity; in *The Book of Common Prayer* it was expressed liturgically, in *The Book of Homilies* (1547) it was expressed warmly and attractively, and in *The Ordinal* candidates for the ministry were asked whether they accepted and would abide by this divine authority.

4. It is an **Evangelical** Way. Inside *The Book of Common Prayer*, and within the primary service of Holy Communion, and in other services as well, is expressed St Paul's doctrine (expounded in Romans and Galatians especially) of Justification by Faith. By this doctrine the apostle explained the Gospel, the Evangel, and how the Good News is "the power of God unto salvation to every one that believeth … for therein is revealed a righteousness of God by faith unto faith" (Romans 1:16–17). There is no doubt but that the first duty of the worshipping Church is to proclaim the Gospel and to share it with all sinners so that they may repent of sin, believe in the Lord Jesus Christ and receive eternal salvation.

5. It is a **Traditional** Way. The Church of England did not ditch everything from its medieval past in the sixteenth century. It conserved and renewed that which was good, and since then has developed its own "traditions." Some of these have stayed around and others, having served for a time, have been dropped. Anglican Churches in other countries have done much the same, according to their own needs and circumstances. The point is that the Church of today receives a living heritage from the Church of yesterday and passes it on refined and reformed to the next generation.

6. It is a **Contemporary** Way. It is a worshipping and serving of the Father through the Son, our Lord Jesus Christ, and with the Holy Spirit now, daily in Morning and Evening Prayer and in consecrated lives. Since Jesus Christ is the same yesterday, today and for ever, and since his Almighty Father is gloriously eternal, Anglicans serve the

living God and know him in love and devotion, even if they use a Bible written millennia ago and liturgies designed centuries ago. When they address God, and God speaks to them, everything is in the present, even if the words and music were composed yesterday, for the Holy Spirit gives life to what God says and provides. Anglicans do not have to use only that which is created today in order to be credible for today, since credibility is provided by the presence of the Holy Spirit, who dwells in human beings as his temples.

Happy is the cathedral, parish church, or mission where all these characteristics are found in a healthy, dynamic, and productive way!

Of course, there have been various major movements through recent history which have deeply affected the ongoing tradition of the Anglican Way as a worldwide phenomenon. Here it will be useful to point to three of these as having left their mark. First of all, there was the Evangelical Revival in the eighteenth and early nineteenth centuries, which left a profound mark on the Church of England and the Churches in colonies and mission fields abroad. Anglicans still sing hymns composed in this revival and support missionary societies created by it. The primary emphasis was upon the duty of each person as a sinner to repent of sin and to believe on the Lord Jesus Christ for the forgiveness of sins and unto eternal life. One general effect of this movement was to underline and strengthen the "Reformed" part of "Reformed Catholicism."

In the second place, there was the Catholic Revival, which began as the Tractarian Movement and became the Anglo-Catholic Movement. Here the "Catholicism" of "Reformed Catholicism" was underlined and emphasized. Rites, ceremonies, church fittings and clergy vestments that belonged to medieval Catholicism, or Continental Catholicism of the nineteenth century, were introduced in modified form into college chapels and parish churches in the late nineteenth century. The primary emphasis was upon the Sacraments as effective means of grace, and to have valid sacraments meant having a rightly ordained and equipped priesthood. Today the use of the word "Mass" for "Holy Communion" and the calling of a clergy-man "Father" are tokens of the influence of this movement.

In the third place, there was the Ecumenical Movement, which in the twentieth century inspired separated Churches to enter into dialogue, to create means of inter-communion, to share common aims, to use similar versions of liturgical texts and creeds, and to attempt to find common doctrine. In general, this movement, especially since the 1960s, has been deeply influenced by the more liberal groups from the member churches and denominations, including the Anglican provinces. It has also, through what is called the Liturgical Movement, produced common texts for use in worship—usually liberal and politically-correct translations. Thus to worship God by means of any modern Anglican liturgy is usually to be using some texts which have been created within this movement.

When an autonomous Province or Church or Communion of Churches possesses some or all the six characteristics noted above, and, further, when it has taken into its life parts of the three movements also noted above, it is not surprising that different members tend to emphasize one aspect of the whole more than others—and, regrettably, sometimes, even emphasize one to the exclusion of others. So there have been what have been called "schools" of churchmanship—e.g., High Church, Low Church, Anglo-Catholic, Evangelical, Latitudinarian, Liberal, Affirming Catholic, Open Evangelical and so on. Sometimes one or another of these schools or parties has sought to dominate in a diocese or even a province, causing others to feel unwelcome. However, in good times it has generally been agreed that the Anglican Way provides the possibility of comprehensiveness, where different schools or parties, possessing a common center, agree to differ in details and expression. The key to any unity is necessarily the common center, which all must share in order for all to belong rightfully together. Until the 1970s this center was the use of the same basic Liturgy of Common Prayer and Ordination Services (howbeit in different languages and with differing ceremonial) and commitment in general terms to the four principles of the Chicago-Lambeth Quadrilateral of 1888. These are the Bible as the rule and ultimate standard of Faith, the two Creeds, the two Gospel Sacraments and the historic Episcopate, locally adapted.

In the new Millennium

It was after the introduction of a variety of liturgies, existing alongside the traditional Book of Common Prayer but often eclipsing it in practice, that the glue that bound the autonomous provinces together in "bonds of affection" began to cease to be sufficient to hold all together in common cause. And it was only from that period of time that Anglicans began to hear more and more about "the Instruments of Unity," which it was hoped would be the new glue to unite all in the continuing "bonds of affection." Here "instrument" is used in its technical sense as "a means whereby something is done" or "a means of pursuing an aim." And the four instruments now generally accepted are: the See [archbishopric] of Canterbury, the Lambeth Conference of Bishops (held every ten years), the Anglican Consultative Council and the Primates' Meeting. None of these has any legal authority and so together they are nothing like the various departments of the Vatican in Rome. Further, any moral authority they may have is a matter of local judgement. They can only recommend and persuade toward unity of mind, heart and action. The Archbishop of Canterbury does, however, have a form of authority in one important sense—he issues the invitations to bishops to attend the Lambeth Conference and so controls who attends. Yet when assembled this Conference has no legal authority to make canon law or official doctrine, for it can only make resolutions and offer reports, and these are not binding on anyone. In brief, it is not a Synod but a Conference; and it is not an Ecumenical Council but a decennial Meeting.

The Windsor Report (2004) from "The Lambeth Commission on Communion," appointed by the Archbishop of Canterbury, has called for further means to seek to bind Anglican provinces together in unity. These include a common covenant which would restrict the possible actions of individual provinces for the common good, an integrated canon law for all the provinces, and increased authority and powers to the See of Canterbury to intervene in provinces other than its own when there are grave problems to solve. But the possible implementation of all this is a decade or more ahead.

I would suggest that a necessary part of any approved common covenant would be the restoration of that which has been effectively lost or forgotten by many especially in the West, the classic Anglican Formularies—that is, the *Book of Common Prayer*, the *Ordinal* and the *Thirty-Nine Articles*. In the rest of this book, I shall seek to explain and commend these Formularies as being, under the authority of the Word of God written, the Bible, still necessary for the integrity and unity of the Anglican Way in the decades ahead.

Perhaps here is the right place to pause for a moment and to reflect on the word "Formulary." This is not a word in common use, but is an important word, nevertheless, as it has been used in serious Anglican discourse consistently since the sixteenth century. The Latin, *formularius (liber)* [= a book of formulae], on which it is based, pointed to a collection of set forms or instructions for the performance or direction of a ceremony or an official duty. Thus a "formulary" within a national Church is a book which contains the set forms and rules of what the Church believes, teaches and confesses, the liturgy it uses, and the way it creates the ordained ministry. In reforming itself in the sixteenth century, the *Ecclesia Anglicana* (the Church of England) reformed its Latin Formularies (those which had been in force in the medieval period) to create three new ones—*The Book of Common Prayer, The Book of Ordination Services* (*Ordinal*) and *The Thirty-Nine Articles*, along with a new edition of Canon Law. Under the final and supreme authority of Scripture, these summed up and presented the standards, norms and means by which the reformed Church of England sought to be the national jurisdiction of the Catholic Church of God. These Formularies not only provided the way to worship and serve God daily, but they also distinguished the Church of England from other jurisdictions. Wherever the Church of England went around the world, either with the British Empire or through missionary work, the Formularies went as well and were translated either in whole or part into over one hundred and fifty languages. The only exceptions to this rule were a few dioceses and provinces created by Anglo-Catholic missions. In these *The Thirty-Nine Articles of Religion* as a Formulary was sometimes minimized or left out.

In the Canon Law of the Church of England, the mother Church of the Anglican family, the doctrinal foundation is stated with clarity in Canon A5:

> The doctrine of the Church of England is grounded in the holy Scriptures, and in such teachings of the ancient Fathers and Councils of the Church as are agreeable to the said Scriptures. In particular such doctrine is to be found in the Thirty-Nine Articles of Religion, the Book of Common Prayer, and the Ordinal.

This indicates that the Anglican Way is at heart a particular way of reading, interpreting and receiving the truths of Holy Scripture as the Word of God written. The use of the ancient Creeds and the Formularies is part of this process of hearing and doing what God declares to his people through his Word.

From the beginning, the Anglican Way of Reformed Catholicism looked to the Bible and to the early Church. This is what Bishop John Jewel said over and over again in his writings in the sixteenth century:

> We have searched out of the Holy Bible, which we are sure cannot deceive, one sure form of religion, and have returned again unto the primitive church of the ancient fathers and apostles, that is to say, to the first ground and beginning of things, as unto the very foundations and headsprings of Christ's Church.[1]

It is important to notice that the Anglican Way does not base its secondary foundation solely upon a Statement of Faith as does for example the Presbyterian Way. Rather, it brings together three different types of Christian and ecclesial literature—a Book of Prayer for public worship, A Book of Ordination Services to make deacons, priests and bishops, and a short Statement of Faith to set forth a doctrinal position in relation to Scripture and to some major controversies in the history of the Church. By doing this it shows that true theology is the art of living unto God the Holy Trinity in faith, hope and love, within the communion of the one, holy, catholic and apostolic Church of God.

In the next three chapters we shall examine in turn, *The Articles*, *The Prayer Book* and *The Ordinal*, before concluding with a chapter on Holy Scripture.

For further reading

The Windsor Report, 2004, Anglican Communion Office, London and Morehouse Publishing, New York, 2004; messages to the Anglican Communion from the Archbishop of Canterbury at www.archbishopofcanterbury.org; *Episcopal Innovations, 1960–2004* (2006), by Peter Toon from The Prayer Book Society of the USA at 1-800-727-1928 or www.anglicanmarketplace.com

---

1 *An Apology for the Church of England*, ed. J. E. Booty, 1963, p.xxxvii

CHAPTER TWO

Reformed Catholicism—The Articles

From the Early Church, Anglicans as Reformed Catholic Christians receive the gift of the three Creeds—Apostles', Nicene and Athanasian. By them they gain clear knowledge of the central truths of the Christian Religion and, in particular, the clear statement in precise terms of the two basic doctrines (dogmas) of the Faith. First, that God, the Lord, is a Trinity in Unity and Unity in Trinity, and, secondly, that Jesus Christ is the Second Person of the Trinity, who for our sake assumed our humanity, became Man, and was henceforth One Person made known in two natures.

Anglicans of today receive no Creed from the English Church of the sixteenth century because the three Creeds without change remained the Creeds of the Church in that period. However, from the second half of that century they do receive a kind of extended creed of the kind that had been, or was being produced, in other parts of Europe at that time. From the Evangelical [Lutheran] Church in Germany came *The Augsburg Confession* (1530) and from the Roman Catholic Church in its Counter-Reform movement came the Decrees of the Council of Trent (1545–63). This extended form of Anglican Creed, of which Archbishop Cranmer with Bishop Ridley were the composers of the first draft, became known as *The Thirty-Nine Articles of Religion*. This document is partially dependent on Lutheran texts for doctrine held in common by the Protestant Churches of Europe; but it charters its own path in doctrine in terms of defining the special nature and characteristics of the National Church of England, with its "Godly Prince" as Governor.

One of Three Formularies

Though *The Thirty-Nine Articles of Religion* as a Statement of Faith has a similar taste, feel and look to the Confessions of Faith produced by the Lutheran and Reformed (Presbyterian) Churches, it does not have precisely the same role and function as they. This doctrinal statement is not to be regarded as *the* stand-alone Confession of Faith of the Church of England and other Anglican provinces, in strict parallel to the sixteenth-century Confessions of Faith of the Lutheran and Reformed Churches. *The Thirty-Nine Articles of Religion*, as already indicated, is one formulary of three and thus it is not as a text free-standing. It exists in the one circle with the other two (*Prayer Book* and *Ordinal*). When men were ordained and later when they were instituted into an official church ministry in the Church of England they had on each occasion to subscribe *ex animo* [from heart/mind] to all three Formularies. And with respect to *The Articles* this means that the subscribers are committed to certain definite doctrines regarded by the Church as orthodoxy, and that this commitment is very much more than the negative position of restraint within the limits of these same doctrines.

Perhaps it is helpful to remember that a standard and required course in theological colleges and seminaries of the Anglican Churches from the mid-nineteenth century up to the 1960s or 1970s was "The Exposition of The Thirty-Nine Articles." And in the same places, there was Daily Morning and Evening Prayer with regular Holy Communion, using services in *The Book of Common Prayer*. Thus, in practical terms two of the Formularies lived together, and they were joined by the third as the men went forth to be ordained by the service in *The Ordinal*. This is why there were so many solid books on *The Articles* published in the second half of the nineteenth and the first half of the twentieth centuries. Regrettably, this required course is rarely offered today and thus modern Episcopal and Anglican clergy have little sense of the content of the basic doctrines of the historic Anglican Way.

Let us very briefly recall the origins of *The Articles*. The text was first composed by Archbishop Cranmer with Bishop Ridley in 1553 in the reign of Edward VI; then it was suppressed during the reign of the Roman Catholic Mary I, to be revived by an act of the Convocation of the Church of England in 1563 in Elizabeth's reign. Modest revision took place, supervised by Archbishop Parker, and the final version, what we call *The Thirty-Nine Articles*, was authorized in 1571 for all clergy to subscribe.

In reading and interpreting *The Articles* in the twenty-first century, I suggest that if we follow the advice of Bishop

Edward H. Browne we shall not go far wrong. In the introduction to his often reprinted book, *An Exposition of The Thirty-Nine Articles*, he wrote:

> In the interpretation of them, our best guides must be, first their own natural, literal, grammatical meaning; next to this, a knowledge of the controversies which had prevailed in the Church, and had made the Articles necessary; then, the other authorized formularies of the Church; after them, the writings and known opinions of such men as Cranmer, Ridley and Parker, who drew them up; then, the doctrines of the primitive Church, which they professed to follow; and lastly, the general sentiments of the distinguished English divines, who have been content to subscribe the Articles, and have professed their agreement with them for now 300 years. These are our best guides for their interpretation. Their authority is derivable from Scripture alone.

Happily there is easy access to the text of *The Thirty-Nine Articles* at the back of *The Book of Common Prayer* (1662 and 1928 editions).

The Articles were adopted in slightly revised form to take account of a different type of national government by The Protestant Episcopal Church of the USA in 1801 and then were bound together with *The Book of Common Prayer* and *The Ordinal* (in the printings of the editions of 1789, 1892 and 1928). So the American Church had the same Formularies as the Church of England from its origins in the 1780s to the late 1970s. Interestingly, *The Articles* are also printed at the back of the American 1979 Prayer Book as a historical document and in very small print.

Certainly *The Articles* are by their origins a sixteenth-century statement of the Faith. So they may be seen as providing a major signpost and guide through the controversies, debates and divisions of the period of the Protestant Reformation and the Roman Catholic Counter-Reformation. They may also, and more importantly, be seen as pointing the way into a Reformed Catholic expression of Christianity that is based on the Scriptures and humbly learns from history and tradition, especially the period of the Fathers, the first five centuries or so, when there was a general unity in the Church in East and West. Further, they may be seen as setting boundaries for this Reformed Catholic Faith, making clear when and where stepping over the line leads into error and heresy, immorality and wickedness.

Let me admit that *The Articles* may seem boring to those who are not enthusiastic to know what is the basis and content of Reformed Catholic Faith. Yet this is not surprising, for we all know that many important documents are boring, unless one has a particular interest in their contents. For example, wills and testaments, marriage settlements, constitutions and canons, are boring for most people but, at the same time, extremely important to others who have a personal or legal interest in knowing what is written therein!

A quick survey of *The Articles* reveals that they contain what may be called the patristic and catholic dogma of God the Holy Trinity, a Trinity of Persons in the One Godhead, and of Jesus Christ, the only begotten Son of the Father, the One Person with Two Natures, Divine and Human. Also they contain what may be called the distinctive doctrines of the Reformation—e.g., the authority of Scripture, its clarity in presenting the message of salvation, the saving and redeeming work of Christ Jesus, the nature of sin, justification by faith issuing in works of love, the vocation of the Church on earth, and the priority as means of grace of the dominical Sacraments of Baptism and the Lord's Supper. To these important themes are added statements concerning the ordaining of clergy, the marriage of clergy, traditions in the church, excommunication, the civil magistrate, possession of property and making oaths. Interestingly, although *The Articles* do not specifically mention *The Book of Common Prayer*, they do specifically refer to The Bible, *The Ordinal*, and *The Books of Homilies*. In the last, we may recall, are found very readable explanations of what the authority and power of Scripture is all about, and also what it means to be justified by faith alone, a faith that works by love and is expressed in faithfulness and good works.

It has been pointed out that *The Articles* were intended to be, and in some sense remain, both pacificatory and denunciatory. On the one hand, they sought by silence or at least by general statements, to calm speculation of the English clergy on mysterious and scholastic questions not settled in Scripture. On the other hand, where there was need to expose errors and heresy this was done, so that from the ministry of the Church of England were excluded both advocates of Romanism and of "Anabaptism" (radical Protestantism), as well as others who did not embrace Reformed Catholicism.

What the three Formularies, together with *The Books of Homilies* and Canon Law, provide for us—as summarized for ordinary folks in the late 16th century by the great Lancelot Andrewes—is a simple 1, 2, 3, 4 & 5 of the Anglican Way. That is, the expression of Christianity known since 1549 as the Religion of the Church of England, and later called Reformed Catholicism and the Anglican Way, is based upon: ONE Canon of Scripture with TWO Testaments, whose basic, doctrinal message is summarized in THREE Creeds (Apostles', Nicene and Athanasian) and in more detail in the decrees and canons of FOUR ecumenical councils [Nicaea (325), Constantinople (381), Ephesus (431) and Chalcedon (451)] and by the general developments (e.g., fixed liturgy, threefold ministry, Church Year, Canon Law and so on) of the first FIVE centuries.

The 1, 2, 3, 4 & 5 are the basis for the Way, not the whole structure; without a foundation there is no structure. Further, numbers one and two are not only first in order but also first in importance. Reformed Catholicism teaches that Councils of the Church may err; and so the creeds and dogmas of councils can never be the primary, solid rock foundation. That must be the Word Incarnate, Jesus Christ, through the Word Written, the Scriptures.

The Articles may be boring to some, even to many, but to those who are committed to exploring, understanding and receiving the Anglican Way as Reformed Catholicism they are exciting and necessary. *The Articles* are certainly not popular with liberal churchmen who do not like, for example, the description of human sinfulness in them; but to those who take the teaching of St Paul in Romans 1–8 seriously they present the truth about human nature—as both sinful and sanctified—with accuracy. Also, *The Articles* are disliked by those who, while remaining Anglicans, hold to certain Roman Catholic teachings on Sacraments and also use an adapted Anglican Liturgy called "The Anglican Missal." Here they are disliked because of their Protestant or Reformed Catholic content and because they are critical of aspects of medieval and sixteenth-century Roman Catholicism. Further, *The Articles* are not popular with some evangelical and charismatic Anglicans who find the doctrines therein not so much wrong but strong, too emphatic, and not user-friendly.

To be a member of the Anglican Way, it is not required that any layman subscribe to *The Articles*, for they were intended for subscription by the clergy and teachers in the Church. The Baptismal and the Visitation of the Sick Services in *The Book of Common Prayer* indicate that what is required of laity as a minimum is commitment to the truths set forth in The Apostles' Creed. Of course, the laity may with the clergy grow into the fullness of orthodoxy found in *The Articles* and the other Formularies, but, strictly speaking, in that the clergy alone have been required to subscribe to them, they are not required doctrinal knowledge for all members. Yet they stand with the other Formularies as the Standard of Faith of the Church of England and most provinces of the Anglican Communion. If you wish to know accurately and in detail what is Reformed Catholicism and the Anglican Way, then you begin with *The Articles* and move on to study also *The Book of Common Prayer* and *The Form and Manner of … Ordaining … Bishops, Priests and Deacons.*

Conversation over the Centuries

We all know that serious dialogue on important matters between Christians of differing backgrounds and convictions can be a good thing, especially when there is mutual respect and a common submission to Christ Jesus as Lord. Likewise, a kind of dialogue or conversation with important Christian teachers and theologians of the past can also be a good thing, especially when the present-day enquirers genuinely wish to discover that which the worthies of the past were seeking to convey by what they wrote. Let us recall that Christian doctrine is not like the theories and hypotheses of the various sciences. Bishops and theologians (not to mention the "faithful") of the fourth or tenth or sixteenth century may well have known more—in devotional, religious and theological terms—about the God and Father of our Lord Jesus Christ and the truth of the Holy Scriptures than, say, a theologian of 1960 or 2006, educated at Oxford and Harvard, and with all kinds of degrees and titles, knows. Let us not doubt that there can be great benefit in seeking to understand and to converse with important, learned and godly teachers of doctrine, piety and holiness, from yesterday.

It would appear—and if true this is good news!—that

today some Anglicans in North America (where regrettably, as we all know, the Anglican Way has lost much of its true character and witness) are beginning to recognize that they can benefit from conversation with the mind and voice of the Church of England, when it spoke and wrote during a period of laying foundations of the Reformed Catholic Way. That is, they are realizing that they can learn from the English Church from the middle of the sixteenth century, specifically through two of its archbishops, Thomas Cranmer and Matthew Parker, and their colleagues. They speak on behalf of the Church of their time, through what we now call the Formularies of the Church of England and of the Anglican Way, not forgetting also the great clarity of the doctrine in the sermons they assembled in *The Books of Homilies*.

There seems to be a growing realization that the doctrinal and moral sustenance gained from modern Anglican liturgies, and from paraphrases or dynamic equivalency versions of the Bible, do not provide anything like the quality and character of the sustenance to be gained from the use of the classic *Book of Common Prayer* and traditional versions of the Bible (e.g., the KJV, ASV and RSV). Using modern liturgies and versions of the Bible has in many cases served to cut well-intentioned people off from historic and orthodox roots, and to plant them in modernity without sure anchors and not truly connected to the central message of the Scriptures and the best insights and traditions of the Anglican Way.

The Anglican Way of Reformed Catholicism is based upon the Word of God written, the authority and supremacy of Scripture, but Scripture as received, preserved, and translated within the catholic Church, not Scripture interpreted by private judgement. So it is the Way which preserves the doctrine and character of the Early Church through its commitment to creeds, dogma, the Threefold Ministry, Liturgical Worship, canon law, government by synods, evangelization and so on. In fact, it has been well said that the genius of the Anglican Way, as it originated in the Church of England between 1549 and 1604, has never been to grow its own theological nourishment, but rather to prepare carefully and wisely what is provided from elsewhere (e.g., from the patristic age, the medieval Church and the Continental Reformation) and to set it attractively and decently upon the table.

Thus it is very clear within the Anglican Way of Reformed

Catholicism, by a study of what Cranmer and Parker actually wrote in the Formularies, what are the essentials of the Christian Faith and Morality and what are the *adiaphora*, the important yet secondary things that are not essential to salvation but useful for the good order of the Church on earth in a particular place and time. Therefore, Anglicans should speak strongly only of those things which are truly central and essential both to Christianity as the true Faith and for the existence of the one, holy, catholic and apostolic Church. Anglican comprehensiveness (in terms of churchmanship) exists within this framework of moderation which distinguishes the major from the minor and does not major on minors. The Anglican Via Media, as it is called, is not half way between Anabaptism (radical Protestantism) and Roman Catholicism; but it is considered moderation in terms of knowing what is essential and what, though good and useful, is not essential.

On a wide area of doctrine and piety, worship and discipline, Cranmer and Parker speak to us and we hear something odd or rare in our times. For example:

we tend to think of morality and ministry in terms of human rights, whereas they think in terms of God's order given in creation to and for man, and known in his statutes, commandments and laws for man;

we tend to think of the immanence of God first (his presence everywhere) and of his transcendence (above and beyond us) in the light of his immanence (and so we tend towards panentheism and pantheism); but they begin with the Majesty of God, his glorious transcendence, and see his presence in space and time in this light;

we tend to think in terms of equality for men and women in all areas life and regard "patriarchy" as a terrible, outdated thing; but they rejoice that God is the Father and that "headship" is given to the husband and father, as well as to the bishop as "father in God," so that they shall exercise generous, gracious rule in home and church;

we tend to think that God accepts us "just as we are" whatever our claimed "orientation" and "impulses;" but they taught that God accepts us just as we are with the purpose of making us different, holy and righteous in his sight;

we tend to think of having a relationship with God which we

can in part negotiate; but they submit to a sovereign Lord who by grace regenerates, justifies, adopts us and makes us his children to display good works to his glory;

we tend to think of the weekly Eucharist as a kind of spiritual fast food that we take when we feel like it or when provided; but for them preparation for Holy Communion in repentance and faith is truly necessary for right reception;

we tend to think that the use of ceremonial, vestments, icons, and explicit symbolism in divine worship is helpful because decorative and aesthetically pleasing; but for them unless these things actually served the Gospel, making it clear, their use was doubtful, not necessary and even harmful.

And we tend to think that to read and meditate upon the Bible whenever we have the time and inclination is just fine, whereas they recognize the duty of devout reading and meditating on Scripture with self examination as a duty to God.

To hear and understand their voice and message and thus engage in this conversation we need devoutly not only to read *The Articles* and to study *The Books of Homilies,* but also to use the classic Prayer Book (e.g. 1662 England, 1962 Canada, 1928 USA) for the Daily Office as a starter. This will put us, as it were, on the same wavelength and enable us to ask and answer such a question as: How did Cranmer and Parker actually approach, read and interpret Scripture and how does this differ from my approach or that of my church? Of course, this is not a one-evening dialogue but a steady conversation over months. But do not be put off. Give it a go! Try it!

Getting People Started

People ask me: How can we get modern evangelical, charismatic and anglo-catholic Anglicans, who wish truly to be "orthodox", to treat *The Articles of Religion* (1571 England, 1801 USA) with the seriousness that belongs to a Formulary of Faith?

Happily, one wiser than I faced this question some twenty-five years ago, and provided the beginnings of an answer in a paper he read to a Conference at King's College, Halifax, Nova Scotia in 1989. The Rev'd Dr Robert D. Crouse suggested that two basic things are required of Anglicans today, if there is ever to be an effective restoration of the authority of *The Articles of Religion* as a Formulary of Faith (along with a related restoration of the authority of Scripture and Creeds).

First, he said, "We must be liberated from that characteristic of modernism (or chronolatry) which regards contemporary opinion as the only valid criterion of truth, and uncritically identifies each new wind of doctrine as 'the leading of the Holy Spirit'." In this regard he suggested that the word of St John is apposite: "Beloved, believe not every spirit but try the spirits whether they be of God" (1 John 4:1).

Secondly, he said, "We must learn to approach our traditional authorities with that spirit of reverent attentiveness which alone will permit them to inform us." That is, our approach must involve an intellectual humility which is ready to listen attentively to the witness of those who have been in Christ before us.

Let us consider these two points. First the problem of Chronolatry. The word "chronolatry" is rarely used, but it is a word that can serve a helpful purpose.[1] *Chronos* is time and *latria* is reverence or worship. So *chronolatry* is the worship of the present, or the placing of the mind and opinions of ourselves or persons today above those of yesterday.

Now in matters purely scientific and concerned with such studies as mathematics, physics and cosmology, the theories of the leading scientists in these fields are obviously to be preferred to those of a former time. And the same applies in other modern scientific study as well. However, the opinions of today are not necessarily better than those of yesterday in all areas of human knowledge and experience.

Regrettably, what is happening today in society, church and culture is that too often we assume that modern opinions about morality and religious doctrine are superior to those of yesterday. In Church synods in the mainline Churches of the USA (Episcopal, Methodist, Lutheran, etc.) there has been an increasing tendency since the 1970s to elevate "contemporary experience" and the "opinions of the elite" above the received tradition of faith and morality, assuming that the latest opinions held by the finest are obviously the best and thus to be made church doctrine!

In this ongoing chronolatry, Church synods, working on

1 It seems to have originated from the pen of the philosopher Jacques Maritain in *Le Paysan de la Garonne* (Paris, 1966, pp. 25–8).

democratic principles (with all the accompanying political activism of working for votes) assume that when they pass a measure, which introduces an innovation (and which is itself usually a rejection of the wisdom of yesterday), then that majority vote is the "leading of the Spirit." In their counting of votes, however, they do not count the saints who have gone before them and who had already "voted" for that which the innovation displaces and replaces!

Have you noticed how both Episcopalians and Methodists now speak of the four-legged stool of theological method— Scripture, Tradition, Reason and *Experience*? In this new formulation (it used to be: Scripture, Tradition and Reason, only) contemporary experience (not only personal and corporate, but also the supposed assured results of the human "sciences") has the final word as to the place and use of the others. And when this door is open, then much that is secular can enter the church baptized in the name of "God."

Chronolatry is a sin. It excludes both the wisdom of the Scriptures and the lesser but still important wisdom of the holy teachers and ecumenical councils of the Church (tradition) from the creation of worship, doctrine and discipline in the present. Not that we are to hide in the past and become irrelevant today, but that we are to exhibit to God and his world that we are members of a people who have received the Faith, and have witnessed to the Gospel, through space and time and that the believers and saints of yesterday also have a vote on what is the Faith for today.

Now, in briefer compass, the second point, the matter of approaching ancient authorities in the right frame of mind. The recognition of authorities always requires on our part an act of faith in them, for the way that genuine learning occurs is from faith to understanding. The ancients knew this well and St Augustine, basing himself on the Latin version of Isaiah 7:9 wrote: "Unless you believe, you will not understand" [*Nisi credideritis, non intelligetis*]. Later St Anselm of Canterbury created the much-used phrase, "faith seeking understanding" [*fides quaerens intellectum*]. We need to approach the Holy Scriptures and *The Thirty-Nine Articles of Religion* believing that in them is wisdom, the wisdom of God and of men, and give ourselves humbly and attentively to their study.

Perhaps the present crisis in the Anglican Communion, over sexuality and the authority of provinces to make their own doctrine, will serve as a catalyst to many, to send us back with humility and attentiveness not only to the classic Formularies of the Anglican Way, but to the chief of all Formularies, the Sacred Scriptures (in a sound translation/ version), to be read and studied by faith seeking for understanding.

For further reading

CD entitled "The Thirty-Nine Articles (Twelve Expositions)" from the Prayer Book Society via www.anglicanmarketplace.com; Oliver O'Donovan, *On the 39 Articles*, 1986; *The Thirty-Nine Articles* (Papers delivered in 1989 in Halifax, Canada, edited by G. Richmond Bridge); and *The Homilies* (edited by Ian Robinson, 2006) from www.edgewaysbooks.com or www.anglicanmarketplace.com

CHAPTER THREE

"That most excellent Liturgy"— The Prayer Book

Recently, the Oxford University Press in America has published *The Oxford Guide to The Book of Common Prayer, a Worldwide Survey* (2006, edited by Charles Heffling and Cynthia Shattuck). Its appearance at the beginning of the third millennium of the Christian era from this prestigious publisher is a testimony both to the importance of *The Book of Common Prayer* in its varied editions since 1549, and to the fact that it remains with us today, still used in many places each week. One strange feature of this comprehensive book is that virtually all the liturgists, who were chosen to write about the history and content of the Prayer Book, are those who have also worked hard to replace this classic Prayer Book with one or another form of "Books of Alternative Services." Then also, those who write about the African provinces freely admit that the classic Prayer Book is still widely used there, while seemingly regretting that this is so! These things noted, it is important to recognize that this Oxford book has much valuable information within its covers, and helps considerably in the study of *The Book of Common Prayer* as a Formulary of the Anglican Way.

In Harmony with Scripture

Over the centuries, since the first edition of *The Book of Common Prayer* (1549), Anglicans have commended and defended this Liturgy in one or another of its editions on the basis of its total harmony with the authority of the Holy Scriptures, the Word of God written. That is, it not only contains large portions of the Scriptures, but its Collects, Prayers, Exhortations and Declarations are informed by and indeed saturated by Holy Scripture. If proof of this be needed then it has been provided in painstaking detail by Henry Ives Bailey in *The Liturgy compared with the Bible* (1850). Further, the doctrines communicated by the liturgical texts are the very doctrines of Scripture and so may be described as biblical teaching.

In stating that the Prayer Book is a Liturgy based on Scripture, Anglicans are not claiming that the way Scripture is used and interpreted in it is uniquely Anglican, and, somehow, superior to the use and interpretation in other branches of the Church. Rather, the claim is that it is the Scripture, and the Gospel it contains, as interpreted by the early Church, and as that interpretation is proclaimed in the Nicene Creed and in the basic Dogmas from the Ecumenical Councils, that is foundational. The decision to use and print in full within the Prayer Book the Eucharistic Lectionary from the medieval "Sarum Use," a Lectionary which went back in content and use to the late patristic era, underlines this claim both to submission to Scripture as God's Word and to the basic way it was read doctrinally in the Early Church.

Anyone who uses either Morning Prayer or Evening Prayer knows that in essence what he is doing is praising, thanking, confessing, supplicating and interceding in God's presence using God's written Word and, at the same time, listening to God's written Word from the lections of the Old and New Testaments. Likewise, he who attends The Order for Holy Communion is aware that he is hearing readings from the Bible, exhortations based upon the Bible, praying in phrases drawn from the Bible and receiving the Sacrament in the context of the repeating of the words of institution by the Lord Jesus.

Anglicans committed to the authority of Scripture have used and continue to use *The Book of Common Prayer* because it allows them to worship the Lord in the beauty of holiness and with spiritual understanding. Of course the Prayer Book is not the Holy Scripture, but it is a well tested way of praying the Holy Scripture in public worship and in a disciplined manner for the whole Christian Year, from Advent to the end of Trinity season.

Since *The Book of Common Prayer* was from the beginning in English, it was in the form of English given it by its editors, primarily by Archbishop Thomas Cranmer. In the providence of God, Cranmer was specially gifted as a writer of English prose and so he provided liturgical texts which stood the test of time and became memorable for thousands, if not millions. What he provided in the middle of the sixteenth century remained the standard English language of Public / Common Prayer until the late 1960s, when experiments in "a contemporary language of prayer" began. The language of the Prayer Book has been highly valued for its pleasing style but, for the discerning, it has been and is valued also for its ability to convey Biblical doctrine through powerful and memorable English. And for any who will make the effort, that language is still evocative and continues to communicate Biblical truth in forms that have a way of lodging in the memory.[1]

The same simple and engaging style also is found in *The First Book of Homilies* (1547). These sermons were written by Archbishop Cranmer and others to help to spread biblical teaching through the Church and were intended to be read by the minister at Holy Communion, if he were unable through lack of theological education to preach a biblically-based sermon of his own creation. I have read some of these homilies at Festal Evensong in English churches, and they were heard and received with a generally warm and appreciative spirit. Though their style and illustrative material are those of the sixteenth century, they are easily understood today and remain powerful communicators of basic Christian teaching. Anyone who reads them today will neither be wasting time nor disappointed!

Years of Desolation

Many Anglicans believe that *The Book of Common Prayer* was first published in 1549, reissued in 1552, and then, in succeeding editions (as authorized by English monarchs beginning with the reign of Elizabeth I) has been used continually to the present day in the Church of England's cathedrals, chapels and parish churches. In response we may say that this belief is not wholly accurate even though it is substantially true; there was one brief period when the Prayer Book was actually banned, and, further, since the 1970s, some parish churches have chosen not to use it except on rare occasions.

From 1559 through to 1645, in the reigns of Elizabeth I, James I and Charles I, *The Book of Common Prayer* was used weekly, often daily, in the cathedrals, churches and chapels of

1 See further, *Neither Archaic Nor Obsolete: the Language of Common Prayer and Public Worship*, by Peter Toon and Louis R. Tarsitano.

England and Wales. Then from 1645 to 1660 under the Long Parliament and then of the Protectorate (Oliver Cromwell and his son) *The Book of Common Prayer* was a forbidden liturgy. With the restoration of Charles II as King in 1660, *The Book of Common Prayer* was restored and thus the edition of this Prayer Book of 1662 became the standard edition that went all over the world, both with the British Empire and also with those sent as missionaries by the various missionary societies of the Church.

Not all the clergy of the Church of England who were in place in 1660 were prepared to accept the use of the Prayer Book. Thus from 1660 to 1662 there was an exodus of nearly 2000 clergy, who, together with the laity who followed them and maintained them, formed what has been called Protestant Nonconformity and Dissent—Congregationalists, Baptists, and Presbyterians. The point I am making here is that England in the middle of the seventeenth century provides an example of a Church that (a) rejects the classic *Book of Common Prayer* for fifteen or so years, and (b) experiments with various kinds of Puritan forms of services, where there was little if any formal liturgy; and then (c) restores the very same Book (in a slightly edited form) that it had used from 1559 to 1645.

And now I ask my reader to recall two things. First, that from the seventeenth century through to the 1970s, the Anglican or Episcopal parishes of the USA used *The Book of Common Prayer*—first in the 1662 edition and then, after Independence, in the American revisions of 1789, 1892 and 1928. Simultaneously, over the border to the north the Canadians also used the same 1662 BCP, as also did the West Indies south of Florida in the islands of the Caribbean. Secondly, that from 1979 The Protestant Episcopal Church of the USA, by the decision of its General Convention, ceased officially to use *The Book of Common Prayer*, as received in this Church and used everywhere in the Anglican Way. The Episcopal Church replaced it with a book of the same name but of a very different content, structure and doctrine. In decisions of 1976 and 1979, the classic *Book of Common Prayer* (known in editions of 1662, 1789, 1892 & 1928) was placed in the archives and a "Book of Varied Services" with varied doctrines was made the Prayer Book and Formulary of the American Anglican province. Interestingly and significantly, Books similar to the American Book were called *Alternative Service Book* and *Book of Alternative Services* in England and Canada respectively. Further, in both places the classic *Prayer Book* was retained with its historic title.

This official absence of *The Book of Common Prayer* from The Episcopal Church has now lasted for nearly thirty years, nearly twice as long as the period it was absent from the Church of England. This is an immense tragedy for the Church and for the United States as a nation. Happily, it has been kept in continual use within this Church by a small number of churches. Further, Oxford University Press has kept in print the 1928 edition, and the Prayer Book Society of the USA reprinted The Altar Edition in 2006 in fine leather.

It is reasonable, I think, to claim that the majority in England between 1660 and 1662 wanted to see the recovery of the use of *The Book of Common Prayer* in their parishes and cathedrals. Regrettably in the new millennium only a very small minority in The Episcopal Church (probably members of the Prayer Book Society of the USA) desire to see a recovery of the American edition of the classic Prayer Book for regular or irregular use on Sundays and Holy Days. The truth of the matter is that the majority of Episcopalians, led by liberal, progressive clergy and liturgists, are content to keep the historic *Prayer Book* and *Ordinal* in the archives securely locked up!

Why? Not primarily because they have wholly rejected the use of "Thou/Thee", for they still sing hymns using this pronoun and some occasionally use Rite I Eucharist and Funeral Service in "traditional language;" rather, because they have rejected the form of Christian Faith, Morality and Order that the historic and classic *Prayer Book* and *Ordinal* represent. Their understanding of the Christian Religion is certainly still communicated by the liberal use of the 1979 Book; but also in the new millennium by other sources: for example, (a) the growing number of modern liturgical texts in the series called *Enriching Our Worship;* and (b) experimental diocesan and parochial rites.

However, there is an active and vocal minority within the Episcopal Church found in parishes and dioceses and known as "The Anglican Communion Network," which claims to be "orthodox." Though attached to the 1979 Book for regular use, it is showing signs (as part of its desire to be accepted by, and acceptable to, the majority of the member churches of the Anglican Communion) of a readiness to recover the historic Formularies as its secondary standards of Faith, with Holy Scripture as the unique and chief authority and foundation.

In looking to go this route, this "orthodox" minority within The Episcopal Church is learning from friends at home and abroad. Overseas, the African Provinces of the Anglican Communion which are most friendly to the cause of this minority are most ready to proclaim that their doctrinal basis is first the Scriptures and then the 1662 Formularies. Within the USA and in "common cause", the Anglican Mission in America and the Reformed Episcopal Church already have the 1662 Formularies as their doctrinal basis.

Let us be honest. The Anglican Way without its classic Formularies is not the Anglican Way but some other way! The Anglican Way cannot be the Anglican Way only with its post-1970s Books of Alternative Services, whatever names they are given.

We can all freely admit that to be a Christian does not require that one be an Anglican, using its forms of worship and living within its discipline. At the same time, we can agree that the Church of God in the world today does not come to us in one form or denomination, but in a variety of forms, some of which are large and some small, some of which have a very long history and others a short one. With around seventy-five million members worldwide, and with a very long history going back through the *Ecclesia Anglicana* to the ancient patristic period, the Anglican Communion of Churches, with its thirty-eight provinces and national churches, can and should offer a viable way of being a Christian within the one, holy, catholic and apostolic Church of God. So also do the stable forms of the Continuing Anglican movement.

The Anglican Way has its distinctive traditions, all of which it claims are subject to revision and reform by the Word of God, the Bible. Central amongst these is the possession of Formularies which define the Anglican Way, but, again, with the proviso that they are subject to the authority of Scripture for defining the way of salvation, faith and conduct. So the Formularies, which took their first English-language form in the mid sixteenth century, have been gently revised on various occasions since 1549 in Great Britain and North America, and also slightly modified / edited as they have been translated into various languages. Yet, to this day, in the constitutions of most provinces of the Anglican Communion, the Formularies remain substantially what they have been and were. Without them, it may be claimed, the Anglican Way is like a boat without a rudder. And it seems to be the case that where their doctrinal and moral content have been abandoned, either legally and practically, or just practically, then the dioceses and provinces which have rejected them present to the world new forms of religion, which have little doctrinal continuity with the historic, traditional, biblically-based Anglican Way.

Alternatives to Common Prayer

From the 1960s, as people in the West became more mobile, experienced greater variety in life, and enjoyed consumer choice, there arose in the Churches a desire for "modern" translations of the Bible (not to replace The King James Version but to exist alongside it) and "modern" forms of Liturgy (not to replace The Prayer Book but to provide an alternative to it). The latter could have been achieved in a conservative way by rendering the whole of the received Liturgy into a form of "contemporary" English, addressing God as "You" not "Thee/Thou." However, the way chosen was for each province, exercising its autonomy, to create new forms of service, different in "shape" and content and often with amended doctrine. When these were eventually collected together in one volume within each province, there existed by the 1980s a growing collection of "Books of Alternative Services" with differing titles and in which were a variety of services and varied doctrines. It may be regretted that there was not universally within the Anglican Communion one basic alternative liturgy to that of *The Book of Common Prayer* but many—due to the polity of the Anglican Communion of Churches wherein each province is independent and autonomous, even if desirous to be inter-dependent.

Facing this situation, attempts were made to give a new definition to Common Prayer. For centuries it had referred to the Services of Public Worship within *The Book of*

Common Prayer and so by extension it also pointed to the Book itself. But with the arrival of new services and the felt need to include them within the title of "Common Prayer," efforts began to make "common" mean "that which has been issued by common authority in a specific place," which of course included *The Book of Common Prayer* and any "Book of Alternative Services." Then other efforts began to reduce common prayer to certain ingredients of liturgical worship that were common to all Rites—e.g., Lord's Prayer, Creed, Gloria, Sursum Corda and so on. The immediate result of all this was the naming of the American Book of Alternative Services, "The Book of Common Prayer," and a later result was the Church of England calling its latest collection of varied services and doctrines, *Common Worship*.[1]

One result of the arrival of the use of a set of related but different Prayer Books was to begin to erase and remove that which had been a primary means of uniting the various provinces and parts of the Anglican Family of Churches—the use of *The Book of Common Prayer* in one or other of its editions, and in this or that language. Until the 1960s travelers could look for an Anglican church anywhere in the world and be reasonably sure that they would recognize its Liturgy, even if in a language they did not speak and using ceremonial which they did not normally experience. After the 1970s, that Liturgy, *The Book of Common Prayer*, was in competition with the modern forms of service and thus it could not any longer be the one glue to bind together the different parts of the Family. And it was in this context, as we have noted already, that the contemporary great emphasis upon "instruments of unity" took shape as a means of providing ways to unite the Anglican Communion of Churches, which was growing in size and diversity. The glue provided by the Prayer Book (and the whole Formularies) had been effectively removed and so, it was hoped, the new adhesive power would come from living persons—the Archbishop of Canterbury, the Lambeth Conference of Bishops, the Anglican Consultative Council and the Primates' Meeting. Unity moved away from being based on common doctrine, common worship/prayer and common ministry (ordained by a common ordinal) and moved towards being

1 For more detail about all this see Peter Toon, *Common Worship Considered*, chapter two.

based on claims to "bonds of affection" with human mediation between and amongst provinces, which possess different doctrine, worship and ministry. (See the latest report on the Anglican Communion *The Windsor Report 2004*, from The Lambeth Commission on Communion.)

A regrettable and sad feature of the introduction of new types and forms of liturgy after the 1960s was that they were sometimes accompanied by attacks on *The Book of Common Prayer* in order to undermine confidence in it amongst clergy and laity and, at the same time, to elevate the supposed superiority of the new Rites. Further, teachers in seminaries and colleges pushed the new Rites on the basis of arguments which now look rather weak or inaccurate. This is made very clear by the content of the second chapter of the recent *Oxford History of Christian Worship* (2005), which presents current academic understanding of liturgy in the Early Church and shows that some of the major assumptions of the creators of the new Services of the 1970s and 1980s were either probably or surely wrong.

However, in the 1980s, thinking that the new Services were soundly based and superior to those in traditional *Common Prayer*, bishops and priests in the dioceses did all within their powers to introduce them, assuming their contemporary relevance and superiority. Very quickly, and more so in some places than others, godly habits of devotion and piety were crushed and communication of Reformed Catholic doctrine and morality was reduced.

Happily, partly in reaction and partly through spiritual discrimination, there is a growing recognition across the Western part of the Anglican Communion that the setting aside of *The Book of Common Prayer* as both Liturgy and Formulary has brought great loss to individual provinces. To restore the use of this Liturgy in its formative editions is, however, not straightforward or easy. One simple problem is that people have got used to addressing God as "You" and using so-called contemporary English in their worship; and their pastors believe that to try to get them to use for their principal services the classic English language of prayer is an impossible task. Whether this is true or false, it is a generally held assumption that few seem to question and even fewer seem ready to oppose. Thus, there is a growing desire to have the historic Liturgy rendered into a form of contemporary

English which preserves the doctrine, content and shape while making it accessible to and acceptable by modern worshippers. To do this satisfactorily is much more difficult than it would appear; yet many believe that it has to be attempted to become a kind of bridge from the land of variety to the land of stability.

A recent Objection to The Book of Common Prayer

One objection to the use of *The Book of Common Prayer* (even if in a carefully prepared contemporary language form) from some modern Anglicans, who are deeply committed to church growth, is based on the claimed fact that it is not "missional". By the use of this recently concocted word they mean "applicable to fulfilling the command of the Lord Jesus Christ to make converts, baptize and teach them" and they are referring to Matthew 28: 16–20. In brief what they are saying is that the traditional Prayer Book is not suitable or appropriate for use in a church that has the priority of evangelization.

To answer this objection, made with the utmost intensity and sincerity, we need to be very clear on certain points. First of all, by its very nature—whether it be from the sixteenth or the twenty-first century—a "Book of Common Prayer" is a Book of Services which the people of God are to use when they meet together for Daily Worship (the Morning and Evening Offices), for weekly Eucharist (the Lord's people at the Lord's Table on the Lord's Day), and for such events as Holy Baptism, Confirmation, Marriage, and Christian Burial. It is a Christian Prayer Book and all its prayers and all its materials presuppose that those who are using it are either baptized, communicant members, or are on their way to being so. It is not a book for those who do not yet believe or are not yet born of the Spirit, but a book of and for the Church of God. It is a book for "insiders" not for "outsiders" although the latter are encouraged to look at it as often as they wish, even as they are also invited to read a good translation of the Holy Bible as often as possible.

Thus its services are not intended to be (in the strict sense) evangelistic, proclaiming the Gospel of God the Father concerning his Son, Jesus Christ, to those who are outside the membership of the one, holy, catholic and apostolic Church, be they Jews, Muslims or pagans. Rather they are the means used by those who have already embraced the Gospel and are maturing in the Faith, in order to worship the Father through his Son, our Lord Jesus Christ, with the Holy Spirit. However, to say this is not to say that the services of Morning and Evening Prayer cannot be adapted and made the basis for a service in which church members invite friends, neighbors and family members to come and experience an act of worship and to hear at its end an evangelistic sermon. (I myself have taken part in many such services when in the Church of England Ministry working in parishes and college chapels.) Also to say the above is not to say that we should not devise special forms of service for evangelistic use outside the normal services of the people of God. This has been done in the past, especially in parish missions, and outreach programs, so-called.

The substantial point here is that the Services in *The Book of Common Prayer* are for the people of God and their purpose is twofold—

(a) to provide the means whereby they can worship the LORD the Holy Trinity, in spirit and in truth and in the beauty of holiness. To adore and worship God is the highest and purest vocation of man, and this vocation precedes the vocation to engage in mission. And to do this in mutual *koinonia* is a taste of heaven on earth;
(b) to provide the means of edification, for maturing in the knowledge and service of God. Services that are well constructed and contain godly doctrine (as those in *The Book of Common Prayer*) build up the people of God for their service of God in his Church and world, and send them forth as pilgrims and sojourners on their way to heaven, to be the salt of the earth and the light of the world on their journey to the new Jerusalem above.

The people of God are to go out from these services as the "sent" people of God, sent by the Lord Christ empowered by his Spirit in "mission."

Now "mission" as used in sacred Tradition, solidly based upon the Bible, is a very large concept. Theologians and Bishops of the Church have spoken of the *Missio Dei*. By this phrase they mean the Mission which begins within the inner life of the Blessed Trinity and leads to and involves the

Mission of the Son, descending from glory to this earth, becoming Incarnate by taking our human nature and making it his own, and his work of revelation, salvation and redemption in this world. Into this massive and glorious mission the Church is called as "a co-worker together with God" as it is indwelt and guided by the Holy Spirit; but it is always first and foremost the Mission of the Holy Trinity by whom the elect are being saved, sanctified and glorified and also by whom the whole cosmos is to be transfigured and regenerated.

In this theological and broad Biblical sense—and not in the restrictive "missional" sense of current times—the whole Liturgy both proclaims and serves the *Missio Dei*! In fact, the biblical presentation of the work of the Father, the Son and the Holy Spirit, echoed in the Prayer Book, is that of one great mission by the Son of descent and ascent, of revelation and illumination, of salvation and redemption, of sanctification and deification, of glory and doxology.

So *The Book of Common Prayer* in its authentic and classic editions wonderfully reflects the *Missio Dei*, and those who use it aright and in godly sincerity, and become co-workers together with God, will be *missional* in the modern sense but engaged also in *Missio Dei* in the larger and thoroughly biblical and theological sense!

For further reading

Peter Toon, *Common Worship Considered*, Edgeways, www.edgewaybooks.com; Peter Toon and Louis R. Tarsitano, *Neither Archaic Nor Obsolete: the Language of Common Prayer and Public Worship*, Edgeways in the UK and the Prayer Book Society in the USA—www.anglicanmarketplace.com; and also from the latter the CD, "The Book of Common Prayer, Six Commentaries," and the CD, "A Special Anglican Trilogy," which contains Bailey's book on the Liturgy and the Bible. The 1928 edition of *The Book of Common Prayer* is available from Oxford University Press of New York City, the Altar Edition based on it is available from The Prayer Book Society, and the 1662 edition is available from both Oxford and Cambridge University Presses in England.

CHAPTER FOUR

"The Form and Manner..." — *The Ordinal*

One of the more interesting writing assignments I fulfilled recently was to engage with three others in producing what has proved to be a widely used text book from Zondervan, with the title, *Who Runs The Church? Four Views on Church Government* (2004). Each of us presented a doctrine of church government and ministry and then each of the others responded to it.

The other three writers, well known in the Evangelical world in the USA, sought to demonstrate that their polity (e.g., Presbyterian or Congregational) was clearly that for which there was a blueprint in the Books of the New Testament. So their presentations were essentially careful Biblical exegesis, for they knew that they could not find clear evidence for their polity in the early or late patristic period. My task was to describe the "Episcopal" form and show its relation to Holy Scripture, its rationale and its place in history. But I did little Biblical exegesis to find the Threefold Ministry of bishop, presbyter and deacon within the books of the New Testament, for I knew that it was not there as a blueprint. I did, however, indicate that there were several examples of a threefold relation—e.g., of apostle, elder and deacon; and, apostle, assistant to apostle (e.g., Timothy) and elders ordained by the assistant. Further, I sought to show that the Church, which actually collected the Books and made them what we call the Canon of the New Testament, was "Episcopal" in structure and that, as such, it was both in harmony with the principles of Church government found in that Canon and also created by the providence of God as a development from the ministry of the Apostles.

One thing is very clear to students of the Early Church: that within a century of the death of the Apostles, the government of the Church by bishops, assisted by presbyters and deacons, was the norm and was everywhere found. Anglicans take this seriously into account in their approach to the government of the Church. Here is what the Committee on the Unity of the Church at the Lambeth Conference of 1930 stated:

> The Episcopate occupies a position which is, in point of historical development, analogous to that of the Canon of Scripture and the Creeds. ... If the Episcopate was the result of a process of adaptation and growth in the organism of the Church, that would be no evidence that it lacked divine authority, but rather that the life of the Spirit within the Church had found it to be the most appropriate organ for the functions it discharged.[1]

In contrast to this approach, there have always been the few, from the seventeenth through to the present, who have believed that the Episcopate and Threefold Ministry are to be clearly found in the apostolic age and within the scriptural testimony.

Ordination in the Anglican Way

In both the Anglican Communion of Churches and the Continuing Anglican denominations, the tradition is of the deacon being ordained by the bishop alone, the presbyter (= priest) being ordained by the bishop, assisted by other presbyters, and the bishop being consecrated by three other bishops, other bishops assisting. Here there are three orders of ministers within the one ordained ministry. In other churches, which were reformed in the sixteenth century and continue today as Protestant denominations, there are usually only two levels of ordained ministry, the deacon and the presbyter. However, in the Roman Catholic Church there is the Threefold Ministry, with the elevation of the Bishop of Rome to the status of "Vicar of Christ on earth."

In modern Prayer Books such as the American Prayer Book of 1979, there are what are called "Episcopal Services." These are for the ordination of a bishop, a priest and a deacon, and they are written in such a way that a man or woman can be ordained using them. In contrast, in *The Book of Common Prayer* there are no services for making deacons, ordaining priests and consecrating bishops. The ordination services for men only and related to *The Book of Common Prayer* are contained in what is usually called *The Ordinal*, and this is normally bound together with the *Prayer*

1 *The Lambeth Conferences, 1867–1948*, Part II, p. 50

Book and *The Articles of Religion*. The full title of *The Ordinal* is, *The Form and Manner of Making, Ordaining and Consecrating Bishops, Priest and Deacons.* In making this a separate book, the Church of England was continuing its own long tradition, since the ordination services in the medieval period were contained in their own specific book, known as *The Pontifical.*

By including *The Ordinal* in its Formularies, the Church of England was making it very clear not only that the ordained ministry is essential to the existence in space and time of the one, holy, catholic and apostolic Church; but that also in the providence of God, this ordained ministry from the earliest times was made up of deacons, presbyters and bishops. Thus the English Church in its new Reformed Catholic existence kept this traditional, threefold ministry, while at the same time it dropped the minor orders of ministry (sub-deacon, acolyte etc.) that were found in the *Ecclesia Anglicana* in the medieval period.

In retaining the traditional episcopate and ministry, the Church of England differed from most of the other regional Churches in Europe, whose new form of existence originated in the Protestant Reformation, and which saw no biblical basis for the distinction between the bishop (*episcopos*) and the presbyter (*presbyteros*). No doubt one of the reasons for the retention of the Episcopate in England was that it was the way in which the "godly prince" chose to rule the Church now that papal supremacy had been removed. In the Preface to *The Ordinal*, Cranmer made a general claim about the origin of the ministry when he wrote:

It is evident unto all men diligently reading holy Scripture and ancient authors [the early Fathers] that from the Apostles' time there have been these Orders of Ministers in Christ's Church: Bishops, Priests and Deacons. Which offices were evermore held in such reverend estimation, that no man might presume to execute any of them, except he were first called, tried, examined, and known to have such qualities as are requisite for the same; and also by public Prayer with Imposition of Hands, were approved and admitted thereunto by lawful Authority. And therefore, to the intent that these Orders may be continued, and reverently used and esteemed, in the Church of England; no man shall be accounted or taken to be a lawful Bishop, Priest or Deacon in the Church of England, or suffered to execute any of the said Functions, except he be called, tried, examined and admitted thereto, according to the Form hereafter following....

In using the expression, "the Form and Manner" in the title, the Church of England was referring to what it learned from the New Testament, the setting aside, or ordaining men, by "the laying on of hands with prayer."

So at the heart of all three services were these two elements, the laying on of the hands of the bishop (with presbyters or other bishops) and prayer. The latter occurred especially through the use of The Litany in which a special suffrage for those being ordained was added. And to emphasize the authority of God's Word written, the Bible, over the Church and especially over its ordained ministry, the newly ordained deacon was given a copy of the New Testament, while the presbyter and bishop received a copy of the whole Bible.

Ordination in the medieval Church

In order to appreciate the changes made in ordination at the Reformation by the Church of England, it will be both interesting and instructive to note briefly the content of ordinations according to the *Sarum Pontifical*, the Latin book used in the medieval period in the *Ecclesia Anglicana*. The ordination of candidates for the minor orders (door-keepers, readers, exorcists, acolytes and subdeacons), and for the diaconate and the priesthood all took place on the Saturday in Ember week and in the context of Mass and after public examination of them. After the ordaining of the subdeacons came the Epistle, then the candidates for the diaconate and priesthood came forward and the Litany was sung. After the Litany the candidates for the priesthood stood aside and those for the diaconate remained. After prayers the bishop laid his hands on each one, saying, "Receive the Holy Ghost." The deacon was vested in the dalmatic; the Book of the Gospels was delivered to him with the words, "Receive authority to read the Gospels in the Church of God, both for the living and the dead." The last deacon to be ordained then read the Gospel, all the deacons retired and the candidates for the priesthood came forward. They received the stole and chasuble; *Veni Creator Spiritus* was sung, all kneeling, and the bishop beginning. After the consecration of the hands of the priests-elect, the paten with oblates and the chalice containing wine were put into them with the words: "Receive authority to offer sacrifice to God, and to celebrate Mass both for the living and the dead." Then the Mass continued and just before the post-communion part, the bishop again laid his hands on each on the new priests, saying, "Receive the Holy Ghost; whose sins thou dost forgive, they are forgiven, and whose sins thou dost retain, they are retained."

The consecration of a bishop took place only on a Sunday and was a rite of much complexity. Before the Mass began, the candidate was examined at length and in detail. After the Gradual he appeared full vested, with the exception of the mitre, the staff, and the ring, and was presented by two bishops to the archbishop. Then came the Litany after which, while two bishops held the Book of the Gospels over the neck of the candidate, all the other bishops touched his head, and the archbishop began to sing *Veni Creator Spiritus.* Then the head and the hands of the bishop-elect were consecrated with chrism and oil. Finally, the staff, ring and mitre were blessed and presented to him and the Book of the Gospels delivered to him, suitable words accompanying each of these *insignia*.

In the Reformed Church of England, the minor orders were abolished, the definition of the priest (and bishop) as one who has "authority and power to offer sacrifice to God and to celebrate Mass for the living and the dead" was dramatically rejected and changed, as we shall see.

The Bishop, Priest and Deacon of The Ordinal *of 1662*

Let us now turn to *The Ordinal* itself and note the high standards required of those to be ordained. "The Form of Ordaining or Consecrating of a Bishop" requires that it take place on the Lord's Day or a Holy-Day. It follows Morning Prayer, includes the Litany and the ancient hymn, *Veni, Creator Spiritus*, and occurs in the context of "The Order for Holy Communion." Before the laying on of hands, there is a thorough investigation of the bishop-elect, and in these questions and answers the vocation of the bishop in the Church is indicated and accepted.

After being asked whether or not he believes himself called to this ministry, the bishop-elect is asked two searching questions about the way that he views, and relates to, the Scriptures and how he intends to use them fruitfully and wisely in his ministry. These questions assume the doctrine of Scripture declared in *The Articles* and *The Homilies* and also that used as the basis of prayer and worship in *The Book of Common Prayer* (see below, chapter five).

The third question also assumes the statement of orthodox doctrine in *The Articles* and expounded in *The Homilies* and asks: "Are you ready, with all faithful diligence, to banish and drive away all erroneous and strange doctrine contrary to God's Word; and both privately and openly to call upon and encourage others to do the same?"

The fourth question gets to the personal life of the bishop-elect, who is called to live "soberly, righteously and godly" and to be "an example of good works to others." Later questions focus on his duty to bring good order, peace and love to his diocese, to care for the poor and needy and to be faithful in the ordaining of deacons and priests.

At the ordination, with the laying on of hands, the archbishop says: "Receive the holy Ghost, for the Office and Work of a Bishop in the Church of God, now committed unto thee by the Imposition of our hands; In the Name of the Father, and of the Son, and of the Holy Ghost. Amen. And remember that thou stir up the grace of God which is given thee by this Imposition of our hands; for God hath not given us the spirit of fear, but of power, and love, and soberness." This form of words assumes that God is present and is actually doing something real and lasting in the life of the new bishop. It also assumes that he has already been ordained to the Ministry of Word and Sacraments as a priest.

Then, giving to the new bishop a copy of the Bible, the archbishop says to him, as a new "Father in God" of the flock of Christ:

> Give heed unto reading, exhortation, and doctrine. Think upon the things contained in this Book. Be diligent in them, that the increase coming thereby may be manifest unto all men. Take heed to thyself, and to doctrine, and be diligent in doing them; for by so doing thou shalt both save thyself and them that hear thee. Be to the flock of Christ a shepherd, not a wolf; feed them, devour them not. Hold up the weak, heal the sick, bind the broken, bring again the out-casts, seek the lost. Be so merciful, that you be not too remiss; so minister discipline, that you forget not mercy:

that when the chief Shepherd shall appear you may receive the never-fading crown of glory; through Jesus Christ our Lord. Amen.

This address both calls the new bishop to live within the message of the Bible and to exemplify its message of mercy in his relation to his flock. (The change from second person singular ["thou shalt'] to second person plural functioning as singular ["you be not remiss..."] occurs occasionally in the Formularies and indicates here that the bishop's relation to God is on the one hand identical to that of all human beings (thou), but that as a member of a particular group (you) he must excel at showing mercy to all, especially the needy.)

"The Form and Manner of Ordering of Priests" also follows Morning Prayer, includes the Litany and *Veni, Creator Spiritus*, and occurs in the context of "The Order for Holy Communion." Before the public examination of the candidates for ordination, the bishop, their "Father in God," delivers to them an Address, which presents what may be called the Reformed Catholic view of the presbyterate. First of all, the demanding duties and responsibilities of this Office are set forth; then it is emphasized what a great treasure is committed to the ordained priest—care of the Body of Christ; this is followed by a statement of the duty of fulfilling these duties by diligent study and renunciation of worldly cares and pursuits; and finally there is an exhortation to pray continually for Divine help.

What follow are a few short excerpts from the Address to convey its biblical character and pastoral care:

> Have in remembrance, into how high a Dignity, and to how weighty an Office and Charge ye are called: that is to say, to be Messengers, Watchmen, and Stewards of the Lord....

> See that you never cease your labour, your care and diligence, until you have done all that lieth in you, according to your bounden duty, to bring all such as are or shall be committed to your charge, unto that agreement in the faith and knowledge of God, and to that ripeness and perfectness of age in Christ, that there be no place left among you, either for error in religion or viciousness in life.

> Consider how studious ye ought to be in reading and learning the Scriptures, and in framing the manners both of yourselves, and of them that specially pertain unto you,

according to the rule of the same Scriptures: and for this self-same cause, how ye ought to forsake and set aside (as much as ye may) all worldly cares and studies.

That ye may be wholesome and godly examples and patterns for the people to follow.

If this Address is compared with those provided in the new Prayer Books, what is very noticeable is how deeply this one is based in Holy Scripture and calls for the highest commitment from the new presbyters.

The questions asked of the candidates for the presbyterate are similar in content to those asked of the bishop-elect. The last one asks whether they will "reverently obey your Ordinary and other chief Ministers, unto whom is committed the charge and government over you." (It is of note that in the ordination service in the American 1979 *Prayer Book* the question about the relation to the bishop comes at the beginning rather than at the end of the questions!)

At the laying on of hands, the Bishop says:

Receive the Holy Ghost for the Office and Work of a Priest in the Church of God, now committed unto thee by the Imposition of our hands. Whose sins thou dost forgive, they are forgiven; and whose sins thou dost retain, they are retained. And be thou a faithful Dispenser of the Word of God and of his holy Sacraments, in the Name of the Father, and of the Son, and of the Holy Ghost. Amen.

Here, as with the consecration of the bishop, it is assumed that the Holy Spirit is present to give ministerial gifts, a central one of which is the authority of Christ to declare the forgiveness of sins to repentant sinners, and to withhold it from the impenitent.

Perhaps here it is appropriate to explain that the Formularies ascribe only unto the God and Father of our Lord Jesus Christ the power of remission of sins. Further, they assume that God only forgives those who are repentant and believe in his promises. Added to this they assert and assume that the priest and bishop have a special power and commission, which other Christians do not have, authoritatively to declare this (divine) Absolution and Remission of sin, for the benefit and consolation of truly penitent souls. The biblical background to all this is the words of Christ in Matthew 16:19 and 18:18 with John 20:22–3.

The presbyter/priest is not called "father" or "father in God" but he is required to promise that "he will fashion his own life and that of his family, according to the Doctrine of Christ." Thus he is to exercise gracious headship in both his own family and in the local congregation of the family of God, the treasure given into his care. In no way, however, is he to be—as was his medieval predecessor—the priest whose primary function was to offer the sacrifice of the Mass. The need for " a sacrificing priest" is clearly denied on the basis of the unique sacrifice of Christ on the Cross in all the Formularies and specifically in the "Homily of the worthy receiving ... of the Body and Blood of Christ." In fact, it is always good to remember that the word "priest" in the *Prayer Book* and *Ordinal* is a contracted form of "presbyter" and not the translation of the Greek "hiereus" or the Latin "sacerdos." The role of the presbyter/priest is in Reformed Catholicism transformed from what was in the medieval period seen to be offering a mediatory sacrifice to that of administering and dispensing the benefits of Christ's passion through Word and Sacrament.

This understanding has been enlarged by some later editions of the Prayer Book (e.g., the 1928 of the USA) to include the understanding (from the Early Church) that the Holy Communion is also a Eucharistic Sacrifice (non-propitiatory) at which the reformed catholic priest leads/presides over the offering of the people (praise, thanksgiving, selves-souls-bodies, alms, oblations). Yet this developed doctrine is still a long way from the medieval doctrine of sacrifice.

As he kneels, each newly ordained priest is given a copy of the Bible by the Bishop who says, "Take thou authority to preach the Word of God and to minister the holy Sacraments in the Congregation ... ." He is to be a minister of Christ to administer the Word of God and the Sacraments of the Gospel.

"The Form and Manner of Making of Deacons" also follows Morning Prayer, and a Sermon, includes the Litany and is in the context of The Order for Holy Communion. In the examination, the candidates for the Diaconate are asked: "Do you unfeignedly believe all the Canonical Scriptures of the Old and New Testament?" and "Will you diligently read the same unto the people assembled in the Church where you shall be appointed to serve?" Further, they are asked whether they will reverently obey their bishop and other senior clergy and whether they will "frame and fashion" their own lives and those of their families so that they will be wholesome examples to the flock of Christ.

The duties of the deacon are stated as: to assist the priest in public worship and especially at the Holy Communion; to read the Scriptures publicly and also sermons from *The Books of Homilies*; to instruct the young people in the Catechism; to assist with Baptisms of infants, to preach (if the Bishop gives a license); and, to engage in pastoral visitation, keeping the priest informed as to the needs of the flock. It is assumed in *The Ordinal* that the deacon will, without ceasing to be a deacon, be ordained priest a year or so after being made deacon, if his life and ministry suggest that this is appropriate.

The Episcopate

It is both important and interesting to note that no special theory or doctrine of the Episcopate is provided in *The Ordinal* or *The Articles* or *The Homilies*. For example, it is not specifically claimed or suggested that the bishops are the successors in space and time of the Apostles. The Episcopate is accepted on the grounds that it originated, developed and appeared in the early Church by the providence of God and remained therein from the first century to the present. Further, and importantly, the nature of the office and its duties, are very much described in biblical terms and doctrines. However, after the Elizabethan Settlement in 1559, great care was taken in the consecration of Matthew Parker as Archbishop of Canterbury to ensure that it fulfilled traditional criteria.

Also, at this early stage in The Anglican Way, there was no sense that those ordained as deacons and presbyters in Continental Europe by the laying on of the hands of presbyters were not truly ordained and also genuine ministers of the Church of God. In fact in the sixteenth and seventeenth centuries such clergy were allowed to minister in the Church of England without being re-ordained by a bishop. Later, in missionary work abroad promoted by Evangelical Anglican missionary societies, men ordained by presbyters only were also employed as ministers of Word and Sacrament in Anglican missions.

However in modern times, the Church of England and the provinces of the Anglican Communion have become more strict in their insistence that to be the licensed minister of Word and Sacrament in a diocese a person must have been ordained by a bishop. And, the doctrinal position of the Episcopate has been accordingly elevated not only in theological writing by individual theologians, but also in both canon law and one short but major pan-Anglican document. In fact, it was in the debates with the Puritans in the late sixteenth and with Roman Catholics in the early seventeenth centuries, that Anglican divines began to develop and clarify views of the nature and vocation of a bishop. Then later, through the work of the Non-Jurors in the eighteenth century, and confirmed by the Anglo-Catholics a century later, episcopacy as such came to be seen by some as part of the very identify of the Church. And this doctrine entered Anglo-Catholic text-books.

Since the end of the nineteenth century, the Anglican Way has been generally committed to what has become known as *The Chicago-Lambeth Quadrilateral of 1886, 1888.* This originated in The Protestant Episcopal Church's House of Bishops meeting in Chicago in 1886 and was then taken to London and approved in modified form by the Lambeth Conference of Anglican Bishops in 1888. Since then it has been much quoted.

The Quadrilateral addresses the theme of unity amongst the historical Protestant denominations (Lutheran, Presbyterian, Methodist etc.) and states that four elements are essential for such unity—the acceptance of the Old and New Testaments as the revealed Word of God; the Nicene Creed as the sufficient statement of the Christian Faith; Baptism and the Supper of the Lord as the two Dominical Sacraments; and the Episcopate. The full definition of the latter is: "The Historical Episcopate, locally adapted in the methods of its administration to the varying needs of the nations and peoples called of God into the unity of the Church." From nowhere in the Formularies could one actually deduce that the Historic Episcopate is necessary for the unity of the Church on earth and this assertion may be taken as a development of doctrine within the Anglican Way.[1]

1 See the comments of Oliver O'Donovan, *On the 39 Articles*, 1986, pp. 118ff.

There used to be discussions about the relation of the Episcopate to the Church in terms of whether it was of the *esse* (very being), of the *plene esse* (the fullness of being) or of the *bene esse* (well being). Roman Catholic theologians went for the highest category of the *very being*, as did also some Anglo-Catholics. High-Church Anglicans went for the *fullness of being* for they did want to assert that Protestant Churches were not within the visible Church of God. Evangelical Anglicans went for the *well being* for while they highly valued the Episcopate in a functional way, they did not think either that it was essential to the existence of the Church or that it necessarily belonged to the Church as it ideally ought to be.

More recently, when modern Anglican theologians think of the Episcopate, explain it to themselves and commend and defend it to Congregationalists and Presbyterians, they usually claim that its importance and strength derive from the combination of the following considerations:

1. The Episcopate symbolizes and secures in an abiding form the apostolic mission and authority within the Church of Christ; historically the Episcopate became in the Early Church the organ of this mission and authority.

2. In early times the continuous succession of bishops in tenure of the various Sees was valued because they secured the purity of apostolic teaching as against, for example, the danger of the introduction of novel and erroneous teaching by means of written or secret traditions, falsely ascribed to apostolic authors. It has remained a function of the Episcopate, even after the era of the promulgation of dogma by Ecumenical Councils, to guard the Church against erroneous teaching.

3. The Bishop in his official capacity and vocation represents the whole Church in and to his diocese, and his diocese in and to the Councils of the Church. He is therefore a living Representative of the unity and universality of the Church.

4. The Bishop in his diocese represents the Good Shepherd; the idea of pastoral care is inherent in his office. Both clergy and laity look to him as Chief Pastor, and he represents in a special degree the paternal quality of pastoral care ("Father in God").

5. In as much as the unity of the Church is in part secured by an orderly method of making new ministers, and the Bishop is the proper organ of unity and universality, he is

the appropriate agent for carrying on through ordination the authority of the apostolic mission of the Church. The Bishop is deacon, priest and bishop, all three in one minister. He shares the diaconate with his deacons and the presbyterate with his priests.

The point being made is that it is the coalescence of all these elements in a single person that gives to the Episcopate its peculiar importance in mature Anglican doctrine. And of course, what is stated above is much more than one can find in *The Ordinal, The Articles* and *The Prayer Book* and represents the influence of what may be called "High Church" and "Anglo-Catholic" theological reflection over the centuries.

In Conclusion

The Ordinal in its English edition of 1662 is very much the ordinal of a Church that is Reformed Catholic, and which, while respecting tradition and historical continuity, is very much desirous of keeping close to the Word of God written. In practical terms, by the use of priestly vestments, by the presenting of more than a Bible to the bishop and priest immediately after the act of ordination, and by the deportment and dress of the bishops and clergy taking part, the Reformed Catholic nature can be made to be less "Reformed" and more "Catholic." It is rather easier to be openly "High Church" and "Anglo-Catholic" and even "Progressively Liberal" with the majority of the recent ordination services, than with *The Ordinal* of 1662; even as it is more difficult to be traditionally "Evangelical/Reformed" with these modern services than with the traditional services. All this said, and recognizing much more could be said about ceremonial, vestments and the ordaining of women, it is *The Ordinal* of 1662 which is the Formulary for the Church of England and most of the Anglican Communion. However, this Formulary can be and has been modified in some provinces not by changing the words within *The Ordinal* itself, but by changing canon law in relation to *The Ordinal*— e.g., by allowing the ordination of women through canon law provision even when *The Ordinal*, in its natural reading and doctrinal assumption of male headship in the family, does not permit it.

Since there has been much debate in recent years over the kind of life that is appropriate for or required of an ordained minister, it will be useful to quote the old Canon C26 of the Church of England in closing.

1. Every bishop, priest, and deacon is under obligation, not being let by sickness or some other urgent cause, to say daily the Morning and Evening Prayer, either privately or openly; and to celebrate the Holy Communion, or be present thereat, on all Sundays and other principal Feast Days. He is also to be diligent in daily prayer and intercession, in examination of his conscience, and in the study of the holy Scriptures, and such other studies as pertain to his ministerial duties.

2. A minister shall not give himself to such occupations, habits or recreations as do not befit his sacred calling, or may be detrimental to the performance of the duties of his office, or tend to be a just cause of offences to others; and at all times he shall be diligent to frame and fashion his life and that of his family, according to the doctrine of Christ, and to make himself and them, as much as in him lies, wholesome examples and patterns to the flock of Christ.

If the ordained ministers do not set godly and holy examples of the dedicated, consecrated and sanctified life, to whom shall the laity look for examples?

For further reading

On the history of *The Ordinal*, see P. F. Bradshaw, *The Anglican Ordinal: its history and development from the Reformation to the present day*, SPCK, 1971; for a discussion of the role of a bishop today see *Bishops—But What Kind?*, edited by P. Moore, SPCK, 1982; and see the Essays on "Ministry and Priesthood" and "Episcopacy" in *The Study of Anglicanism*, edited by Stephen Sykes *et al.*, SPCK, revised edition, 1998.

CHAPTER FIVE

One Canon, with Two Testaments: The Word of God Written

The doctrine which is most central to the Protestant Reformation of the sixteenth century is the final authority of Holy Scripture for faith and conduct. Upon the teaching and content of the Scriptures the Reformers attempted to rebuild the Church of God and renew the way of Salvation. Certainly justification by faith alone is most important in terms of the message of salvation by grace; but, it is only so because it is the clear teaching of the New Testament, especially the Letters of St Paul. Beneath this doctrine, as a solid foundation, is the authority of the Bible, which is set forth in all three Formularies and in *The Books of Homilies*, with consistency and care.

First, however, in terms of methodology, let us note that, only after declaring the common, received Faith of the Church, in God the Holy Trinity and the One Lord Jesus Christ, Incarnate Son of the Father, do *The Articles* turn to the Bible. This is because, to put it formally, the Order of Reality (that which truly is) comes before the Order of Knowledge (how and where we find the One who truly is, Reality). Article VI is entitled, "Of the Sufficiency of the holy Scriptures for salvation." Here, after an important declaration, the Books of the OT are all listed individually (so that the OT and the Apocrypha are not conflated as in the Roman Catholic Church); but the Books of the NT which are assumed to be known and accepted by all, are not listed individually. The declaration is as follows:

> Holy Scripture containeth all things necessary to salvation; so that whatsoever is not read therein, nor may be proved thereby, is not to be required of any man, that it should be believed as an article of the Faith, or to be thought requisite or necessary to salvation.

In contrast, the books of the Apocrypha are useful for instruction in morality and behavior. They are not to be regarded as authoritative for establishing what is to be believed as the Christian Faith. So these books are read a

51

little in the Daily Lectionary for the Offices, but they are not part of the Eucharistic Lectionary. Yet Canticles from the Apocrypha are used in the Daily Offices.

The Canon

As the list of books of the New Testament was agreed by all the Churches, so also was the authority of the New Testament, as a principle, agreed in the sixteenth century. What needs to be stated, for it is not so obvious, is the authority of the Old Testament as Holy Scripture. This is the topic of Article VII, which addresses the subject from the perspective of "law." This is a fruitful way of relating the two Testaments as one Canon. For to speak of "law" is to speak not only of eternal realities ordained by God, Creator, Judge and Redeemer, but also, of laws, rules and regulations which belong to, and are required within, any society of people living in space and time in an ordered way: therefore, to speak of "law" is to be able to speak of both (a) that which abides for ever, and also (b) that which passes away when no longer required. In this context, Article VII makes the following claims:

1. There is no opposition between the Old and the New Testaments in terms of their central message from God.
2. In both Testaments "everlasting life is offered to mankind by Christ, who is the only Mediator between God and man."
3. Those who teach that the OT "fathers" (Abraham, Jacob, Moses etc.) looked only for promises from God concerning salvation in this world of space and time—e.g., promises concerning the possession of a land with an appointed king and a fruitful economy with deliverance from local and international foes—are wrong. For, included in God's message to them were promises of eternal salvation.
4. The moral law recorded in the Old Testament is to be obeyed by Christians; but the Mosaic Law in the Torah concerning ceremonial, ritual and civil matters is no longer in force for the people of the new covenant. These parts of the Torah belonged only to the old covenant dispensation, which having been fulfilled in Christ Jesus, no longer applies to Christian activity and behavior.

Practically speaking, since the Old Testament is read systematically morning and evening in the Daily Offices, it is most important for clergy and people reading it to know why it is the Word of God. The Law and the Prophets spoke of the

Messiah, the Christ, and, of course, the New Testament declared his full identity and described his words and work. And in Christ, and Christ alone, is salvation from God. (Perhaps it is useful to notice in passing here that one of the claims made by those who believe that so-called homosexual partnerships are morally acceptable is that one cannot clearly separate, as does this Article, the moral law from the ceremonial and dietary regulations in Leviticus. Therefore, if the Church today is to cite Levitical texts as moral law in favor of the prohibition of sodomy and same-sex partnerships, then it also should cite Levitical texts, that occur within the same context, to prohibit the use of certain types of food or social customs. The answer to this charge cannot be presented in full here for it requires consideration of the place of law in any given society, here Israelite society, and the relation of that law to the order of creation and the purpose (the good) for which mankind was created—and for this I commend the discussion by Oliver O'Donovan in his book, *On the 39 Articles*, 1986, pages 63–4.)

So, why is Scripture authoritative? Because of its unique message which is centered upon Jesus the Christ and declares the gift of everlasting life through, in and with him. It contains all things—the information, ways and means—that are necessary for eternal salvation; that is, of bringing sinful men living in an evil age into the full redemption and glory of the kingdom of God of the age to come, through, in and with Jesus Christ the only Savior. This unique information is found absolutely nowhere else. And, very importantly, the authority of this message in the words that it is provided is objectively true without any reference to methods of interpretation. God has given to the world a means, a way, and an order of knowledge concerning his relation to us as the Savior and Redeemer. This order of knowledge, this way whereby we may know what he is saying and giving to us, is the Holy Scripture, nothing less and nothing more. It is the Bible, first of all in its original languages, and, secondly, in faithful translation into the vernacular. This is why one of the first acts of reformation in the Church of England was placing a large English Bible in every parish church of the land.

It is important to note that what is taught and declared in Articles VI and VII is not the order of Reality but the order of knowledge. The Scriptures are not the real, eternal Word itself, which is the Person of our Lord Jesus Christ, who alone is the Reality and by whom alone there is everlasting salvation. Rather the Bible is the God-given order of knowledge, the ordained and ordered means by which we hear of, and are encountered by, the Reality, the Lord Jesus Christ. The Bible is the Word written, not the Incarnate Word himself. If there is Bibliolatry in any evangelical fundamentalism in the twenty-first century, there is none in the Anglican Formularies.

First and foremost, then, the Holy Scriptures are the unique order of knowledge by which we encounter the Reality, the Word made flesh, and salvation in him, and in him alone. And it is, therefore, Jesus Christ, the Son of God incarnate, whom we encounter in the Old Testament in the sustained and continuous reading of the Daily Lectionary; and it is the same Jesus Christ, now truly present amongst us, whom we encounter in the New Testament in the Daily Lectionary. Likewise, it is the one and the same Word made flesh who encounters us in the Epistle and Gospel of the Eucharistic Lectionary for Sundays and Holy Days.

Since the Holy Scripture is the unique order of knowledge, a major discipline of the Anglican Way is to read the Bible prayerfully and meditatively daily in order to know and receive the fullness of the message of salvation. Public hearing of the reading of Scripture is a means of grace from God. There is no sermon appointed by *The Book of Common Prayer* for the Daily Offices, but only in "The Order for Holy Communion" on the Lord's Day and high festivals. Thus by each and by all the basic way to salvation (which includes living by faith in faithfulness and love) may be known through the daily hearing and/or reading of the Bible. Nowhere is this made clearer than in the Homily on Reading Scripture, written by Archbishop Cranmer, and found in the *First Book of Homilies*, with the title, "A Fruitful Exhortation to the Reading and Knowledge of Holy Scripture."

Cranmer thoroughly believed in the transforming power of the Scriptures and wrote these words at the beginning of this homily:

> Unto a Christian man there can be nothing either more necessary or profitable than the knowledge of holy Scripture; forasmuch as in it is contained God's true word, setting forth his glory and also man's duty. And there is no

truth nor doctrine necessary for our justification and everlasting salvation, but that is or may be drawn out from that fountain and well of truth. Therefore as many as be desirous to enter into the right and perfect way unto God must apply their minds to know holy Scripture; without the which they can neither sufficiently know God and his will, neither their office and duty.

He continued by stating what is true objectively but also what he had experienced personally:

And, as drink is pleasant to them that be dry, and meat to them that be hungry, so is the reading, hearing, searching and studying of holy Scripture to them that be desirous to know God or themselves, and to do his will. ... These books [of Scripture] therefore ought to be much in our hands, in our eyes, in our ears, in our mouths, but most of all in our hearts. For the Scripture of God is the heavenly meat of our souls; the hearing and keeping of it maketh us blessed, sanctifieth us, and maketh us holy: it turneth our souls: it is a light lantern to our feet: it is a sure, stedfast, and everlasting instrument of salvation: it giveth wisdom to the humble and lowly-hearted: it comforteth, maketh glad, cheereth and cherisheth our consciences: it is a more excellent jewel or treasure than any gold or precious stone: it is more sweet than honey or honeycomb; it is called "the best part," which Mary did choose; for it hath in it everlasting comfort.

In short, "the words of Scripture be called 'words of everlasting life', for they be God's instrument, ordained for the same purpose. They have power to turn through God's promise, and they be effectual through God's assistance; and being received in a faithful heart, they have ever an heavenly, spiritual working in them."

In *The Second Book of Homilies* there is a second sermon on the topic of Holy Scripture, though not written by Cranmer but probably by Bishop Jewel. Here is one short exhortation from it:

Let every man, woman and child therefore with all their heart thirst and desire God's holy Scriptures, love them, embrace them, have their delight and pleasure in hearing and reading them; so as at length we may be transformed and change into them. For the Holy Scriptures are God's treasure house, wherein are found all things needful for us to see, to hear, to learn, and to believe, necessary for the attaining of eternal life.

Here we notice again the absolute centrality of the Scriptures in and for the Christian Religion and for the gift of eternal life.

The Formularies

Let us turn now to *The Ordinal*, where we find this question is asked of the candidates for ordination to the presbyterate (priesthood):

> Are you persuaded that the holy Scriptures contain sufficiently all doctrine required of necessity for eternal salvation through faith in Jesus Christ? Are you determined out of the said Scriptures to instruct the people committed to your charge, and to teach nothing (as required of necessity to eternal salvation) but that which you shall be persuaded may be concluded and proved by the Scriptures?

Having answered in the affirmative, the candidate also promises "with all faithful diligence, to banish and drive away all erroneous and strange doctrines contrary to God's Word," and "to frame" his own life and that of his family, by the same Word of God written. Immediately after ordination he is given a Bible and told to "Take authority to preach the Word of God ... ." In the consecration of a bishop similar questions are asked and promises made. Further, as "Father in God" of the flock of Christ, the bishop is also asked:

> Will you faithfully exercise yourself in the same holy Scriptures, and call upon God by prayer, for the true understanding of the same; so as ye may be able by them to teach and exhort with wholesome doctrine, and to withstand and convince the gainsayers?

After being consecrated, he is given a Bible and told to "give heed unto reading, exhortation, and doctrine. Think upon the things contained in this Book. ..."

It is rather important to realize that for Reformed Catholicism the Bible is not "Two Testaments making One Canon" but "One Canon with Two Testaments." Today we are so used to the existence of departments of Old and New Testament in seminaries and colleges, and to their working in parallel rather than as one, that we find it hard to think from the unity of Scripture, the one continuous set of books which constitute God's Word written, to its being made up of two testaments. Rather we tend to think of two different collections of books which are bound together but read and studied separately, except on infrequent occasions.

But let us go back to the Formularies and to the place of interpretation of the Scriptures in the Church as seen by Arch- bishops Cranmer and Parker. In Article VIII "Of the Three Creeds", the Apostles', Nicene and Athanasian are named, and then it is stated "they ought thoroughly to be received and believed." Why?—"for they may be proved by most certain warrants of Holy Scripture." That is, the Church in her long reading of the Bible over the centuries has found that the basic dogmas of the Trinity and the Person of Christ stated in these Creeds are faithful elucidations and statements of the Faith that is presented dynamically and usually in the common-sense mode in the content of the texts of the books of the Bible. Thus, these teachings (doctrines, dogmas) are also helpful, in turn, in the continual reading of the Scriptures, for they supply to the faithful a kind of mindset through which the message of eternal salvation in the Bible becomes the clearer in the daily reading thereof.

In Article XX, "Of the Authority of the Church", there is a clear rule of interpretation provided:

> The Church hath power to decree Rites and Ceremonies, and authority in Controversies of Faith; and yet it is not lawful for the Church to ordain anything that is contrary to God's Word written, neither may it so expound one place of Scripture, that it is repugnant to another. Wherefore, although the Church be a witness and a keeper of holy Writ, yet, as it ought not to decree any thing against the same, so besides the same ought it not to enforce anything to be believed for necessity of salvation.

Here it is assumed that it is not the solitary individual but the Church, through her ordered persons and means, which interprets the Bible in terms of creating doctrine and morals. Further, the basic unity of the whole canon of Scripture, Old and New Testaments, is assumed here as a given, on the basis that its single Author is God himself. Thus, because of this unity, there will not be teaching in one place that contradicts teaching in another place; rather, differences will be complementary aspects of truth, or insights into truth, within the historical relation of God to his people in the old and then the new covenants of grace.

Also the Church is seen as the guardian of the Scriptures,

preserving them intact in space and time, with the duty before God of requiring as sound doctrine and morals only that which is clearly present and taught within Holy Scripture. Thus the Church has the authority to create, and require in use, a *Book of Common Prayer* and also, having such a book, the authority to revise it. Also it has the authority to hold hearings and give decisions when conflict and controversy arise— always of course based on the clear teaching of the Bible.

In passing we may note that the Church has lost its position as the guardian of the Scriptures in the USA and western world. Within the capitalist market system, publishers assemble their own teams to translate the Bible for a specific market and so there are not just a few versions but something like a hundred available, most of which now are dynamic equivalency renderings, so that they are marketable in and for the specific constituencies of the religious supermarket of the West.

Let us be clear that what is assumed by the Formularies in general, and by Articles VI and XX specifically, is, first of all, an essentially straightforward, literal translation of the Bible from the original languages of the kind provided by the King James Version; secondly, with respect to this and based upon it, both the readability and the clarity of the Scriptures concerning the message of salvation in the name of Jesus Christ and the godly life flowing from this salvation, that is basic faith and morals. Thirdly, to this basic clarity to be perceived by all, who read in sincerity of faith and submission to the Lord, is added the duty of the Church to teach, in its sound doctrine and morals, what this salvation means in practice for daily living as the body of Christ in the world, and for each child of God in faith and faithfulness within the household of God. The Church must always be governed by the Scripture and not Scripture by the Church! Further, the Church must be careful not to mishandle or manipulate Scripture without regard for the unity of God's Word written, and for the analogy of faith (*analogia fidei*), according to which the cardinal doctrines of the faith are clearly revealed in holy Scripture; and thus passages that are difficult or subject to controversy must not be interpreted (a) in a manner contrary to those cardinal doctrines, or (b) discordantly with what is plainly taught elsewhere in holy Scripture.

The Articles do not teach the modern, popular doctrine of the right of private judgement in the interpreting of Scripture. There is certainly a duty and right to read the Bible within the context of prayer and seeking after God; but, there is no encouragement to interpret privately and independently past the point of the accepting of the clear message of salvation by and in Christ. Only in one Article (XXXII) is there any hint of the right of private judgement and that is the right of the deacon, priest or bishop to choose to marry.

The Church (catholic and national) has the duty both of deciding what is clearly taught in the Bible and then also of what may be deduced from what is clearly taught therein. We have already noted that *The Articles* accept the use of the three Creeds in the churches, and these are used in catechizing and in worship, because their content expresses the central doctrines of the Bible, as these are known by the Church which continually reads the books of holy Scripture. This usage points to the generally favorable attitude of the *Articles*, *Ordinal* and *BCP* to the teaching and basic institutions of the early Church before its split into East and West, and when it was seeking to be subject to the authority of Scripture. So together with the Creeds is accepted the monarchical Episcopate, with the orders of presbyter and deacon (see Article XXXVI, "Of Consecration of Bishops and Ministers" and the Preface to *The Ordinal*). It is not claimed that the Threefold Ministry is clearly taught and required by Scripture. Rather, it is said to have been in place since ancient times and to be agreeable to the teaching of Scripture with regard to oversight and teaching in the Church.

On the other hand, some matters are clearly taught in the Scriptures and so the Church speaks clearly and reverently about them. Such, for example, are the following doctrines found in *The Articles*:

the Atoning death of the Lord Jesus Christ (II and XV);

the bodily Resurrection and Ascension of the same Lord Jesus (IV);

the "two sacraments ordained of Christ our Lord in the Gospel, that is to say, Baptism and the Supper of the Lord" (XXV, XXVII and XXVIII);

the doctrine of justification by faith by the grace of God in Christ, and good works as the fruit of saving faith (XI, XII, and XIII);

the inability of man because of inbred sin to save himself (IX and X);

the predestination to eternal life of God's elect, chosen in
  Christ (XVII) and,
the right of deacons, priests and bishops to marry (XXXII).

Further, what is clear in Scripture as divine teaching is
placed within the public services of worship of the Church as
found in *The Book of Common Prayer*. If one examines "The
Order for Holy Communion" what is taught in the Articles
concerning the Holy Trinity, the Lord Jesus Christ, the
Atonement, the sinfulness of man, the nature of justification
by faith and the Gospel Sacraments is set forth in doxology,
in praise, thanksgiving and prayer.

There is one more important way in which Scripture is
authoritative for the people of God in worship, and this is
rarely spoken of or explained these days. Already we have
noticed how the daily reading of the Old and New Testaments in Morning and Evening Prayer is the initial and proper
way for people to encounter the Word of God written. To this
encounter, we need to add another one, and this is the Eucharistic Lectionary, those portions of holy Scripture appointed
for the Epistle and Gospel through the Christian Year. These are
not random choices of biblical passages but were put together
around the fifth century or earlier to communicate essential
doctrines of the Christian Faith concerning our Lord Jesus
Christ and salvation and sanctification in his Name. There is
a natural division at Trinity Sunday. From Advent to Trinity
Sunday there is a great emphasis on Dominical Holydays,
and thus of the manifestation of the Lord Jesus in space and
time, who he is and what he is, which are the foundation of
Faith. After Trinity Sunday we enter the non-festal part of the
Christian year where the emphasis is on what Jesus and his
apostles teach us about the Christian life.

In conclusion

In concluding, we see how the Church in the Anglican Way
has a most intimate relation to the Holy Scriptures as the Word
of God written. The Church stands under the apostolic
testimony presented in the New Testament and is obligated
by the apostolic testimony. Why? Because the Church was
created by the apostolic testimony; and to be the Church is to
be formed, molded and guided by that testimony, living in it,
by it and from it. And that written testimony comes by God's
appointment with its preparatory testimony, the scriptures of

the old covenant, and this one canon with two testaments is the Christian Bible.

The Church is the Church of God the Father and of the Lord Jesus Christ and, therefore, it is under the authority of the Scriptures, the divinely appointed sphere where what God has revealed, taught and done is presented to those with eyes to see and minds to receive. The Church engages with the Scriptures daily in the Offices and weekly in the Order for Holy Communion to learn first of all the way of salvation and everlasting life in Jesus Christ, and then the doctrine and morals which flow from this spring of life. At the same time, the Church preserves the text of the Scriptures and translates them, as and when required, into local languages, so that the people of God can hear the Word of God addressed to them in a form they can understand. Further, the Church as a corporate body has the duty to teach the people of God the doctrine that is clearly taught in the Scriptures, and also what may be clearly deduced from that same clear teaching in terms of doctrine and duty.

In the Preface to *The Great Bible* (1539), placed in every parish church in England, we can read these words, penned by Cranmer:

> All manner of persons, of whatever estate or condition they be, may in this Book learn all things what they ought to believe, what they ought to do, and what they should not do, as well concerning Almighty God, as also concerning themselves and all others.
>
> For the Holy Ghost has so ordered and fitted the Scriptures to their task that in them innkeepers, fishermen and shepherds may find their edification, as great scholars their erudition: for those books were not made to vain-glory, like as were the writings of the Gentile philosophers and rhetoricians, to the intent the makers [writers] should be had in admiration for their high styles and obscure manner of writing, whereof nothing can be understood without a teacher or an expositor. But the apostles and prophets wrote their books so that their special intent and purpose might be understood and perceived of every reader, which was nothing but the edification or amendment of the life of them that read or hear it.

While there is a clarity to much of Holy Scripture, at the same time, there are portions that are difficult to understand. Cranmer recognized this and in the first Homily wrote: "Scripture is full, as well of low valleys, plain ways and easy for man to use and to walk in, as also of high hills and mountains that few men can ascend unto." So it is that the clearer parts of Scripture will cast light upon those covered by darkness and those parts that are difficult will be interpreted by those that are easy to understand. Again as Cranmer put it: "There is no thing spoken under dark mysteries in one place, but the self same thing in other places is spoken more familiarly and plainly, to the capacity of the learned and unlearned."

Let us now join Archbishop Cranmer, not preaching but praying. The relation of the Church to the Word of God written is most clearly presented in Cranmer's composition in the Collect used on the Second Sunday in Advent by *The Book of Common Prayer* and addressed to the Father of the Lord Jesus Christ.

> Blessed Lord, who hast caused all holy Scriptures to be written for our learning; Grant that we may in such wise hear them, read, mark and inwardly digest them, that by patience and comfort of thy holy Word, we may embrace and ever hold fast the blessed hope of everlasting life, which thou hast given us in our Saviour Jesus Christ. Amen.

Here is the Anglican charter for not only reading the Bible but also meditating upon its message; and for not only meditating on its message but also receiving that message into one's heart and life.

Finally, here is the closing appeal from the second Homily on Scripture, from which we have already taken a quotation:

> God, therefore, for his mercy's sake, vouchsafe to purify our minds through faith in his Son Jesus Christ, and to instill the heavenly drops of his grace into our hard stony hearts, to supple the same; that we be not contemners and deriders of his infallible word, but that with all humbleness of mind and Christian reverence we may endeavour ourselves to hear and to read his sacred Scriptures, and inwardly so digest them, as shall be to the comfort of our souls and sanctification of his holy Name. To whom with the Son and the Holy Ghost, three Persons and one living God, be all laud, honour, and praise for ever and ever. Amen.

The Anglican Way is certainly identified, recognized and known through its three Formularies and its Books of Homilies, but it ought to be more fully identified, recognized and known through its submission to God the Holy Trinity by means of his revealed and written Word, the Holy Scriptures.

Epilogue: Three Formularies

To maintain and use the three Formularies, as the distinctive Anglican means and ways of being subject both to the Lord Jesus Christ, the Word made flesh, and to the Holy Scriptures, the Word written, and thereby retaining the Reformed Catholic nature and characteristics of the Anglican Way, is a high privilege and solemn duty. And it is placed before both the Churches of the Anglican Communion and the Continuing Anglican Jurisdictions at this momentous time in the history of Anglicanism.

To be committed to the Formularies is not to live in the past or to avoid modern knowledge, insights and issues; but it is to see them, as the Creeds and doctrinal statements from the Church of the Fathers, as living tradition, which, though of the past, is also of the present. Perhaps the illustration of the old fashioned wheel with its hub at the center, its spokes going out from the center and ending at the circular rim will help. Commitment to the Formularies is to be fastened securely to the hub and not to go past the rim in order to preserve unity in comprehensiveness. Too often Anglicans take their spoke as it were through the rim and out into no-man's land when they major on minors, secondary matters, of things which belong to other traditions!

It may be said that guided by the Formularies, the Church of the Anglican Way, in its Reformed Catholic Faith, will always, by God's help and guidance display these characteristics:

Worship and serve the Father through his Incarnate Son and with the Holy Spirit, because it is believed that God the Father revealed himself and provided salvation through the same Son and Holy Spirit. Thus the Church will knowingly, deliberately and thankfully always be committed to a dynamic Trinitarian Theism.

Regard and treat the Holy Scriptures as the unique authoritative Source of knowledge of God's salvation and of his will for the Church and the world. Therefore the Church will always read the Scriptures publicly and privately as the Word from heaven and it will always be prepared to be reformed and renewed by the same Word of God.

Be wholly committed to and preach the Gospel of salvation by grace through faith and not by human effort or works.

Thus it will not support or commend anything that suggests or implies that human beings can save themselves from sin by being and doing good; and it will have as a priority the missionary mandate of Matthew 28:19–20.

Provide the Sacrament of Baptism to the children of believers and to converts to Christ; and celebrate the Sacrament of the Lord's Supper for baptized believers of the flock of Christ: and do so in the way that Christ commanded and taught.

Call the people of God of the flock of Christ to lives that are different in quality from those around them, lives that adorn the Gospel and display the fruit of the Holy Spirit. Thereby the Church will be the salt of the earth and the light of the world.

Engage in Daily Prayer and Biblical Meditation through the disciplined and habitual use of Morning and Evening Prayer.

Only use contemporary services for church worship and evangelistic outreach that are doctrinally in harmony with the Formularies and that do not dumb-down, modify or change the truths of God's Word.

Maintain the Threefold Ministry as a biblically-defined ministry so that under Christ the Lord and Shepherd it may be the living means of good order and holy example in the Church and also of the edification and sanctification of the faithful.

Be genuinely comprehensive in terms of churchmanship, as long as the variety is securely fastened to the foundations, and each school or party is truly a credible form of the Anglican Way.

Watch and pray, knowing that the Second Coming of the Lord in glory to judge the living and the dead, draws near and that his people on earth, as aliens in the evil world, are to be engaged in his work when he arrives.

Only God, the Holy Trinity, knows what is the future of the Anglican Way as part of the one, holy, catholic and apostolic Church in space and time. The duty of Anglicans is not to seek to know the mind of God as to the future, but to be authentically Christian in their Anglican profession of faith and morality, prayer and duty, mission and service.